D0605992

COMPACT *Research*

Bulimia

Diseases and Disorders

ReferencePoint
Press®

San Diego, CA

Other books in the Compact Research Diseases and Disorders set:

Anorexia
Anxiety Disorders
Bipolar Disorders
Depressive Disorders
Impulse Control Disorders
Mood Disorders
Obsessive-Compulsive Disorder
Personality Disorder
Self-Injury Disorder

*For a complete list of titles please visit www.referencepointpress.com.

Bulimia

Peggy J. Parks

Diseases and Disorders

ReferencePoint
Press®

San Diego, CA

© 2013 ReferencePoint Press, Inc.
Printed in the United States

For more information, contact:
ReferencePoint Press, Inc.
PO Box 27779
San Diego, CA 92198
www.ReferencePointPress.com

ALL RIGHTS RESERVED.
No part of this work covered by the copyright hereon may be reproduced or used in any form or by any means—graphic, electronic, or mechanical, including photocopying, recording, taping, web distribution, or information storage retrieval systems—without the written permission of the publisher.

Picture credits:
Cover: Dreamstime and iStockphoto.com
Maury Aaseng: 33–35, 47–49, 61–63, 75–77
© Henry Ruggeri/Corbis: 12
© Ragnar Schmuck/Corbis: 17

LIBRARY OF CONGRESS CATALOGING-IN-PUBLICATION DATA

Parks, Peggy J., 1951–
    Bulimia / by Peggy J. Parks.
       pages ; cm. -- (Compact research series)
    Audience: Grade 9 to 12.
    Includes bibliographical references and index.
    ISBN 978-1-60152-502-4 (hardback) -- ISBN 1-60152-502-8 (hardback)
    1. Bulimia--Popular works. I. Title.
    RC552.B84P37   2013
    616.85'263--dc23
                                                  2012036631

Contents

Foreword

❝Where is the knowledge we have lost in information?❞

—T.S. Eliot, "The Rock."

As modern civilization continues to evolve, its ability to create, store, distribute, and access information expands exponentially. The explosion of information from all media continues to increase at a phenomenal rate. By 2020 some experts predict the worldwide information base will double every seventy-three days. While access to diverse sources of information and perspectives is paramount to any democratic society, information alone cannot help people gain knowledge and understanding. Information must be organized and presented clearly and succinctly in order to be understood. The challenge in the digital age becomes not the creation of information, but how best to sort, organize, enhance, and present information.

ReferencePoint Press developed the *Compact Research* series with this challenge of the information age in mind. More than any other subject area today, researching current issues can yield vast, diverse, and unqualified information that can be intimidating and overwhelming for even the most advanced and motivated researcher. The *Compact Research* series offers a compact, relevant, intelligent, and conveniently organized collection of information covering a variety of current topics ranging from illegal immigration and deforestation to diseases such as anorexia and meningitis.

The series focuses on three types of information: objective single-author narratives, opinion-based primary source quotations, and facts and statistics. The clearly written objective narratives provide context and reliable background information. Primary source quotes are carefully selected and cited, exposing the reader to differing points of view, and facts and statistics sections aid the reader in evaluating perspectives. Presenting these key types of information creates a richer, more balanced learning experience.

For better understanding and convenience, the series enhances information by organizing it into narrower topics and adding design features that make it easy for a reader to identify desired content. For example, in *Compact Research: Illegal Immigration*, a chapter covering the economic impact of illegal immigration has an objective narrative explaining the various ways the economy is impacted, a balanced section of numerous primary source quotes on the topic, followed by facts and full-color illustrations to encourage evaluation of contrasting perspectives.

The ancient Roman philosopher Lucius Annaeus Seneca wrote, "It is quality rather than quantity that matters." More than just a collection of content, the *Compact Research* series is simply committed to creating, finding, organizing, and presenting the most relevant and appropriate amount of information on a current topic in a user-friendly style that invites, intrigues, and fosters understanding.

Bulimia at a Glance

Bulimia Defined

Bulimia is an eating disorder whose primary characteristic is bingeing on large amounts of food and then purging in an attempt to rid the body of excess calories.

Purging and Nonpurging Behaviors

Self-induced vomiting and abuse of laxatives and/or diuretics are common methods used by bulimics to rid the body of excess calories. Other methods involve nonpurging behaviors such as excessive exercise and fasting between eating binges.

Prevalence

An estimated 1.5 percent of females and 0.5 percent of males in the United States are believed to suffer from bulimia.

Behavioral Symptoms

The most obvious signs of bulimia are an obsession with body size and weight gain, eating abnormally large amounts of food in one sitting, and making trips to the bathroom soon after eating.

Physical Symptoms

Signs of repeated forced vomiting include broken blood vessels in the eyes, damaged teeth, thinning hair, puffiness in the cheeks, and calluses or scrapes on the knuckles or backs of hands.

Combination of Causes

Scientists believe that multiple causes contribute to bulimia, including genetics, personality traits, emotional issues, and the media's focus on thinness.

Health Risks

Bulimia can cause stomach ulcers, chronic constipation, damage to internal organs, and imbalances of essential minerals known as electrolytes; the latter can lead to heart problems and death from heart attack.

Prevention

Experts say programs that address the risks of bulimia could potentially prevent the disorder, but such programs are much rarer than those that focus on drug and alcohol addiction and obesity.

Overcoming Bulimia

A number of treatment methods can help sufferers recover from bulimia, but the majority of those afflicted never seek help; also, studies have shown that the death rate among bulimia patients is twice as high as that of individuals without eating disorders.

Overview

66 Bulimia is more than just a problem with food. It's a way of using food to feel in control of other feelings that may seem overwhelming. 99

—Office on Women's Health, an agency of the US Department of Health and Human Services.

66 Individuals with bulimia overvalue thinness and rate their self-worth based on the size and shape of their bodies. 99

—Massachusetts General Hospital Harris Center, which is dedicated to the understanding, prevention, and treatment of eating disorders.

Lady Gaga is as well known for being eccentric and outrageous as she is for her singing and songwriting, and she is wildly popular—so much so that many people are taken aback to learn how insecure she was as a teenager. During a February 2012 presentation to a group of girls at Brentwood High School in Los Angeles, the singer (whose real name is Stefani Joanne Angelina Germanotta) was brutally honest about her difficult teenage years, including her struggle with bulimia. In response to a student's comment about how confident and assured she seemed to be, Lady Gaga replied: "I used to throw up all the time in high school. So I'm not that confident." She went on to explain that her self-induced vomiting originally started as a futile attempt to make herself look like the thin girls at her school: "I wanted to be a skinny little ballerina, but I was a voluptuous little Italian girl whose dad had meatballs on the table every night."[1]

When asked how she was finally able to overcome bulimia, Lady

Gaga answered that she had a very specific motivation. "It made my voice bad. So I had to stop. The acid on your vocal chords—it's very bad." She spoke freely of her own experience because she wanted to get a message across to young women: that they need to be aware of how the media unrealistically glorify physical beauty, thinness, and perfection. "Every video I'm in," she said, "every magazine cover, they stretch you; they make you perfect. It's not real life. I'm gonna say this about girls: The dieting wars have got to stop. Everyone just knock it off. Because at the end of the day, it's affecting kids your age. And it's making girls sick."[2]

What Is Bulimia?

The practice of gorging on food and then vomiting afterward is a primary characteristic of bulimia nervosa (bulimia). Those who suffer from the disorder consume abnormally large amounts of food in a very short period of time—as much as five thousand calories in just one hour. To alleviate their guilt and shame over losing control, while also attempting to rid their bodies of calories, they force themselves to vomit. This purging, as it is known, may lessen tension and provide a sense of relief for bulimics. Any good feelings are very short-lived, however, and are soon replaced by self-disgust, guilt, and shame.

Purging most often involves self-induced vomiting, but bulimics also use other methods to rid their bodies of food. Many abuse laxatives or diuretics (substances that increase urination), and/or use enemas to force bowel movements. They may also use nonpurging methods, such as excessive exercise or fasting. It is not uncommon for people with bulimia to use a combination of methods. One day they may gorge on food and then force themselves to vomit, and the next day they exercise frenetically for hours at a time. This was the case with recovered bulimia sufferer Jessica Setnick. After she discovered bingeing and purging, she got a summer job at a fitness center and became obsessed with exercise. She writes, "I could work out as much as I wanted—all day long, and after

> " The practice of gorging on food and then vomiting afterward is a primary characteristic of bulimia nervosa (bulimia). "

Lady Gaga, known worldwide for her outrageous costumes and performances, suffered from bulimia as a teenager. During a visit to a Los Angeles high school in 2012, she discussed her teenage obsession with being skinny and the self-induced vomiting she hoped would make her thin.

hours, too. I was logging about 50 hours of exercise a week at that point. Extreme physical activity often goes hand in hand with bulimia."[3]

The Deeper Problem

Bulimia is commonly perceived as a way of achieving thinness and the perfect body, but the real problem goes much deeper. Mental health professionals say that even though bulimia patients do want to be thinner, psychological problems are at the root of the disorder. One who agrees with that perspective is April Uffner, who developed bulimia when she was thirteen and struggled with it throughout high school. "For sufferers," says Uffner, "struggling with their weight is only the tip of the iceberg. Underneath, they are tangled in a web of emotional issues, behaviors and compulsions that are ruining their health, bodies, and ironically their looks."[4] People with bulimia often suffer from low self-esteem and lack the ability to cope with the normal problems and stressors of life. They are often perfectionists who find it impossible to live up to their own unrealistic expectations.

Another characteristic of bulimia is the distorted way sufferers tend to view their own bodies. Most are desperately unhappy with their body size and shape, and this is true whether they are overweight, of normal weight, or even too thin. Such a flawed perception of one's actual size is one of the biggest problems associated with bulimia, as sufferers are incapable of seeing themselves as they really are. This was true of recovered bulimia sufferer Taylor Ellsworth, who saw herself as "glamorous and beautiful" even though she was dangerously thin. She writes: "My hipbones jutted out from the pasty white flesh of my abdomen and air breezed between my thighs. My elbows bumped against my ribs every time I moved my arms and none of my clothes fit." Yet Ellsworth did not see the emaciated girl in the mirror. Because of her desperate quest to be thin, she was convinced that she looked better than ever. Now, when she looks at photographs of herself taken during that time, she can see how truly distorted her image of herself was." "My eyes were puffy, my face gaunt, my hair stringy and thin, and my skin deathly white," she says. "I looked like Lindsay Lohan in the infamous mugshot taken the night she was arrested for DUI [Driving Under the Influence] and cocaine possession."[5]

Spiraling Out of Control

Bulimia is a difficult, emotionally painful disorder for anyone who struggles with it. At first, bulimics often have the distorted idea that self-induced vomiting is a convenient way to keep from gaining weight while still being able to eat their favorite foods. Purging may initially be viewed as an option to be used only after eating too much. Over time, though, eating binges and purging become more and more frequent, and sufferers are caught in a cycle from which they find it impossible to escape. The American Psychological Association explains: "Once people start engaging in abnormal eating behaviors, the problem can perpetuate itself. Bingeing can set a vicious cycle in motion, for instance, as individuals purge to rid themselves of excess calories and psychic pain, then binge again to escape problems in their day-to-day lives."[6]

> " Although bulimia has been shown to affect people of all ages, ethnicities, and walks of life, it is difficult for health officials to know how many actually suffer from it. "

This destructive pattern soon spirals out of control, as Uffner knows from personal experience. Bulimics eventually become addicted to food, hate themselves for being unable to control their eating, and purge on a regular basis, often numerous times each day. Uffner writes: "The disease is like a raging monster inside them that they are no match for. Most bulimics are caught in a cycle, they don't want to be the way they are. The problem is, their bodies are used to these patterns, and it is very hard to stop."[7]

Prevalence Estimates

Although bulimia has been shown to affect people of all ages, ethnicities, and walks of life, it is difficult for health officials to know how many actually suffer from it. Statistics are typically based on reported cases, so these numbers are skewed because most sufferers never seek help. Population studies can help determine the prevalence of a particular disease or disorder, but isolating for bulimia in this type of research is rare. One of the few national studies, conducted by researchers from Harvard Medical School, was published in February 2007. The team found that 1.5 percent of females and 0.5 percent of males in the United States had suffered from bulimia at some point in their lives.

For a study published in March 2011, researchers analyzed the results of a comprehensive national survey of 10,123 adolescents that was conducted between February 2001 and January 2004. Based on this analysis, the team determined that bulimia affected 0.9 percent of teenagers aged thirteen to eighteen. The gender breakdown was similar to that of the 2007 study: 1.3 percent of adolescent females and 0.5 percent of adolescent males have suffered from bulimia sometime during their lives.

These studies have shown that bulimia affects females at more than twice the rate of males, although the data could reflect incomplete statistics. According to many eating disorder specialists, males typically view eating disorders as a "female problem" and may be too ashamed to tell anyone or seek help. But bulimia is widely believed to be nondiscriminatory, affecting males and females of all ages. Says the Office on Women's Health, which is a branch of the US Department of Health and Human Services: "It is true that most bulimics are women. . . . But bulimia affects people from all walks of life, including males, women of color, and even older women."[8]

Warning Signs

Symptoms of bulimia are not always obvious to family members or friends. Those who suffer from the disorder typically go out of their way to hide their binge eating and purging from others, as the American Psychological Association explains: "Often acting in secrecy, they feel disgusted and ashamed as they binge, yet relieved of tension and negative emotions once their stomachs are empty again."[9] Eventually, though, the signs of bulimia start to become noticeable. These include an obsession with body size and weight gain, eating abnormally large quantities of food in one sitting, trips to the bathroom immediately after eating (so the person can vomit), and/or excessive exercising.

The physical symptoms of bulimia may also not be apparent at first, but as time goes by they become more obvious. Signs of self-induced vomiting include broken blood vessels in the eyes, teeth that look clear due to destroyed enamel, rashes on the skin, and enlarged salivary glands that cause puffiness in the cheeks, which is a condition referred to as "chipmunk cheeks." Another symptom of frequent vomiting is scrapes and calluses on the backs of the hands and knuckles caused by the teeth, when sticking fingers down the throat to induce vomiting.

Different Disorders, Common Traits

Because the fundamental characteristic of anorexia nervosa (anorexia) is self-starvation, people may have no idea that it affects many of those who have bulimia. It does, however, in an alarming number of cases. Studies have shown that an estimated 50 percent of bulimia patients also suffer from anorexia. And despite how different the disorders may seem, they actually share some of the same traits, such as the obsession with being thin. Referring to bulimia sufferers, the National Institute of Mental Health (NIMH) writes, "Like people with anorexia nervosa, they often fear gaining weight, want desperately to lose weight, and are intensely unhappy with their body size and shape."[10] Another common trait is that people with anorexia and/or bulimia have distorted views of their own bodies.

> " Repeated binge- ing and purging can take a devas- tating toll on an individual's body. "

Krista Barlow struggled with bulimia and anorexia throughout high school and college, and she is convinced that "poor self-perception and body image" were at the root of both. Her bout with anorexia began at the end of her freshman year of high school, when she "slowly stopped eating without anyone really noticing." The bulimia, Barlow says, "started as an accident." She explains: "Once I realized that making myself vomit does not hurt like it does when you have the flu or you're sick . . . it was an easy release for me when I felt stressed or upset. I controlled my food intake with purging."[11]

What Causes Bulimia?

As is typical of most mental disorders, the exact cause of bulimia is unknown. In fact, most scientists are convinced that multiple causes are involved, as the National Association of Anorexia Nervosa and Associated Disorders (ANAD) writes: "There isn't one conclusive cause of eating disorders. Multiple factors are involved, such as genetics and metabolism; psychological issues—such as control, coping skills, trauma, personality factors, family issues; and social issues, such as a culture that promotes thinness and media that transmits this message."[12]

The ANAD's reference to culture and media exemplifies one of the most widely discussed—and controversial—theories about bulimia: that societal pressure and the media play a significant role in its development. Even though the disease is complex and involves much deeper issues

*An irrational, distorted view of body size and weight is one of the charac-
teristics of bulimia. Most of those who suffer from bulimia are incapable of
seeing themselves as they really are.*

than merely the desire to be thin, many experts are convinced that the "skinny-equals-beautiful" perspective is a strong contributor. Says the National Eating Disorders Association (NEDA):

> Media messages screaming "thin is in" may not directly cause eating disorders, but they help to create the context within which people learn to place a value on the size and shape of their body. To the extent that media messages like advertising and celebrity spotlights help our culture define what is beautiful and what is "good," the media's power over our development of self-esteem and body image can be incredibly strong.[13]

What Are the Risks of Bulimia?

Repeated bingeing and purging can take a devastating toll on an individual's body. Physical effects range from a chronically inflamed sore throat to persistent constipation, destruction of tooth enamel, loss of hair, abnormally low blood pressure, and the development of stomach ulcers. Of all the effects of bulimia, none is more dangerous than altering the body's balance of electrolytes. These are essential minerals such as sodium, calcium, and potassium, and if they are out of balance (either too high or too low), the person is at risk of having a heart attack.

"
Mental health professionals say that even though bulimia patients do want to be thinner, psychological problems are at the root of the disorder.
"

People with bulimia may also suffer from a number of psychological effects. They often struggle with a great deal of emotional pain because of their shame and embarrassment, disgust over the way they look, and the feeling that their lives have spiraled out of control. Thus, many develop depression, severe mood swings, and/or anxiety disorders. Personal relationships can also suffer, as Princeton University Health Services explains: "Because bulimics have difficulty trusting people, they have few or no satisfying relationships, and lacking proper coping mechanisms, they do not handle stress gracefully."[14]

Prevention Efforts

Mental health professionals overwhelmingly agree that avoiding bulimia before it develops is preferable to treating it afterward. Yet prevention programs designed specifically for eating disorders are much less common than those for drug and alcohol addiction. Even programs that address obesity are far more prevalent—but some of these programs might benefit people who are at risk of developing bulimia.

One program, Planet Health, is a school curriculum for middle school students that promotes healthy eating and exercise. The idea behind the program is that diabetes, high blood pressure, and other obesity-related diseases that affect adults can potentially be avoided if children learn about the importance of healthier lifestyles. For a report published in 2011, a team of researchers from Atlanta and Boston analyzed the results of a previous two-year trial that involved students from ten middle schools. The Planet Health program was shown to significantly reduce the lifestyle behaviors that led to obesity. Because such behaviors are often precursors to the development of bulimia, the researchers deduced that bulimia in this population would likely also decline. In the 2011 report, the authors explain that "the findings of this study provide additional argument for integrated prevention of obesity and eating disorders."[15] To help reduce the risk of bulimia among adolescents, the research team strongly recommends that prevention programs such as Planet Health be implemented in schools throughout the United States.

> **Prevention programs designed specifically for eating disorders are much common than those for drug and alcohol addiction.**

How Bulimia Is Diagnosed

Although doctors can often recognize bulimia based on interviews with the patient, as well as obvious physical symptoms, there is a specific protocol for arriving at an official diagnosis. The first step is a complete physical examination. According to the Mayo Clinic, the patient will often undergo a series of tests to check for problems such as chronic intestinal conditions, damage to bones, and heart irregularities. These tests are followed by a psychological examination, during which the patient is asked questions about emotional issues, eating habits, body image, and attitude toward food, among others.

Criteria for an official bulimia diagnosis have been established by the American Psychiatric Association. The group includes these criteria in its *Diagnostic and Statistical Manual of Mental Disorders (DSM)*, of which the most recent edition was published in 2013. The three main criteria for diagnosing bulimia include repetitive bingeing by eating abnormally large amounts of food, the feeling that one's eating is out of control, and the habit of ridding the body of excess calories by self-induced vomiting, misuse of laxatives, diuretics, enemas, fasting, or excessive exercise. The *DSM* also specifies that bingeing and purging occur at least twice a week for three or more months, and feelings of self-worth are overly influenced by body shape and weight.

> "The biggest hurdle for most bulimics is that shame, embarrassment, and fear can prevent them from seeking help."

Can People Overcome Bulimia?

The biggest hurdle for most bulimics is that shame, embarrassment, and fear can prevent them from seeking help. As a result, the majority of bulimia sufferers are never treated. Says clinical psychologist Lavinia Rodriguez: "To recover, the individual must acknowledge and accept that food and eating are not the problem. Fears must be confronted, usually with the help of an expert guide. And the bulimic must accept that recovery is a process that requires dedication and hard work. The person must want to be free of the disorder, seek professional help and put recovery first."[16]

For those who do reach out for help, recovery from bulimia is definitely within reach. Treatment programs are designed on an individual basis, depending on a patient's unique needs. They typically include a combination of methods, such as one or more forms of psychotherapy along with antidepressants such as Prozac. The NIMH explains:

To reduce or eliminate binge-eating and purging behaviors, a patient may undergo nutritional counseling and psychotherapy, especially cognitive behavioral therapy (CBT). . . . CBT helps a person focus on his or her current problems and how to solve them. The therapist helps the patient learn how to identify distorted or unhelpful thinking patterns, recognize, and change inaccurate beliefs, relate to others in more positive ways, and change behaviors accordingly.[17]

The NIMH adds that CBT that is specifically tailored for bulimia sufferers is effective at changing binge eating and purging behaviors and attitudes about eating.

A Troubling Disorder

People with bulimia suffer from a variety of problems, both emotional and physical. At first they may view binge eating and purging as a way to shed unwanted pounds, but before long they become addicted to a very dysfunctional, unhealthy lifestyle. If they can manage to face how harmful their behavior is, they may have taken the first step toward overcoming the disorder. With the right treatment program, many can go on to live happier, healthier lives.

What Is Bulimia?

66Bulimia is an eating disorder, but it has little to do with eating. In reality, bulimia has more to do with low self-esteem, perfectionism, unrealistic expectations, anxiety, fear of losing control, depression and other psychological barriers.99

—Lavinia Rodriguez, a clinical psychologist who specializes in eating disorders.

66The cycle of overeating and purging can quickly become an obsession similar to an addiction to drugs or other substances.99

—Melissa Conrad Stöppler, a physician from San Francisco, California.

British psychiatrist Gerald Russell is known for giving bulimia nervosa its name as well as for publishing the first scientific paper on the disorder in 1979. His interest in bulimia began in the early 1970s. Russell saw a number of patients who had previously been diagnosed with anorexia, but who did not seem to fit the diagnostic criteria. Like anorexics, they were all obsessed with being thin. What differentiated them from the skeletal anorexia patients Russell had seen, however, was that they were all of normal or above-normal weight. Among this group, which he referred to as "atypical, difficult, anorexic patients,"[18] another commonality was that they all vomited on a regular basis, which was not a typical characteristic of anorexia.

Russell continued to be perplexed over the mysterious disorder, so he turned to his colleagues for help, as he explains: "I would present these cases at conferences as I wanted advice on how to treat them. They vomited or took laxatives, and they failed to respond to the ordinary measures for anorexia nervosa." What Russell did not figure out until much later was that the patients were purging because they had binged on food beforehand. "If I tell colleagues or students now that I knew the patients were vomiting, but I didn't know that they were bingeing beforehand, they don't believe me," he says. "They say I must have been very blind—or stupid—not to have seen that."[19]

A Modern Disorder

Russell found the missing piece of the bulimia puzzle in 1975, when a patient who was desperate for help visited him. She was a physician and knew that she could be frank and honest with Russell about her problem. "She said something to me which led me to a sudden clarification, an epiphany," he says. "Simply: 'You should know that the reason I vomit is simply to get rid of all this food I eat.' 'Curious,' I thought, and wrote it down, including details of the huge quantities of food she would ingest. I had not thought of that."[20]

Russell was intrigued by the woman's revelation, so he went back to review the records of previous patients. Although he had not made the connection before, he found that their vomiting indeed followed bouts of binge eating. That proved to be the inspiration for his naming the disorder *bulimia nervosa*, which is rooted in the Greek words *bous*, meaning "bull" or "ox," and *limos*, meaning "hungry." "So it means 'hungry like an ox,'" says Russell, "or 'so hungry you could eat an ox.'"[21] He also developed diagnostic criteria for bulimia: an irresistible urge to overeat followed by self-induced vomiting (or purging), coupled with a morbid fear of becoming obese.

> " Many people who suffer from bulimia describe themselves as being addicted to binge eating as well as to the purging that inevitably follows. "

Today Russell is an emeritus professor of psychiatry at the University of London in the United Kingdom. Based on his extensive research, he has concluded that bulimia is a relatively new disorder that only emerged in the 1960s. Although some cases of bulimia-like illnesses were recorded in medical literature in the past, the patients differed from bulimics in important ways, as Russell explains: "They were usually unfortunate people who suffered from even more serious, severe and complicated symptoms—they had other problems, as well as the eating disorder." To further his understanding of bulimia, Russell examined age-specific studies of patients and was able to see that the disorder affected primarily those who were born after 1959. He explains: "This work suggested that whatever it was that made bulimia nervosa more common affected these young women around a crucial time when they were between 18 and 30, and this coincided with the 1960s."[22]

Hopelessly Addicted

Many people who suffer from bulimia describe themselves as being addicted to binge eating as well as to the purging that inevitably follows. They may desperately want to stop, even vowing that they *will* stop, but the disorder controls them more than they control it. This was the case with a young woman named Amy, who constantly struggled with her weight and tried everything possible to get thinner. During one of her attempts to control her eating, she went on a liquid diet and promised herself that she would stick with it. Hunger soon crept in, however, and Amy was overwhelmed with food cravings that she could no longer ignore. Eating disorder specialists Melinda Smith and Jeanne Segal continue Amy's story:

> She grabs a pint of ice cream out of the freezer, inhaling it within a matter of minutes. Then it's on to anything else she can find in the kitchen. After 45 minutes of bingeing, Amy is so stuffed that her stomach feels like it's going to burst. She's disgusted with herself and terrified by the thousands of calories she's consumed. She runs to the bathroom to throw up. Afterwards, she steps on the scale to make sure she hasn't gained any weight. She vows to start her diet again tomorrow. Tomorrow, it will be different.[23]

The addictive nature of bulimia was the focus of a study by researchers from Tufts University School of Medicine in Boston. In reference to the criteria for addiction disorders established by the American Psychiatric Association (APA), the team concluded that bulimia meets all of them. In the study report, which was published in June 2012, the authors write: "Even using the more conservative criteria, BN [bulimia nervosa] meets the definition for an addiction disorder." The authors go on to cite one of the main criteria for substance addiction: tolerance, which is defined as a need for increased amounts to achieve the desired effect or significantly diminished effect with continued use of the same amount of substance. This has also proved to be the case with bulimia, as they write: "Bulimia nervosa individuals also report increases in binge size from onset of their disorder, and tolerance may be responsible for escalating intake."[24]

> Although advocacy organizations and mental health professionals widely agree that bulimia is most common among girls and women, they emphasize that the disorder is not unique to females.

Another of the APA's criteria for addiction is that addicts need larger and larger amounts of the substance and/or use it for a longer period of time than they intended. According to the Tufts group, this is also a characteristic of bulimia, as they explain: "During a meal, individuals with BN may try to eat smaller portions, but end up eating much larger amounts than intended, transitioning them into a binge." Other traits shared by drug addiction and bulimia include withdrawal symptoms, repeated unsuccessful efforts to cut down or control use, and interference with one's social, occupational, or recreational activities. In the conclusion of the report, the authors write that "bulimia nervosa individuals clearly possess propensities for addiction as demonstrated by the significant association between bulimia and substance abuse."[25]

Not for Women Only

Although advocacy organizations and mental health professionals widely agree that bulimia is most common among girls and women, they emphasize that the disorder is not unique to females. According to the

ANAD, an estimated 1 million boys and men in the United States suffer from bulimia. The actual number is likely higher, as males are believed to be much more reluctant to admit that they have a problem than females. In her book *The Parent's Guide to Eating Disorders*, therapist Marcia Herrin writes, "The face of eating disorders has changed and is continuing to change. I have worked with many boys and men, as well as young people representing a diverse set of backgrounds. An eating disorder is now an equal-opportunity disease."[26]

> "
> **The United Kingdom's former deputy prime minister, [John] Prescott publicly announced in 2008 that he had struggled with bulimia for two decades.**
> "

Herrin goes on to say that an important new development in the field of eating disorders is the acknowledgement of experts that the number of men and boys suffering from these disorders is much higher than previously thought. "Where once it was believed that about 10 percent of eating disorder sufferers were male," she says, "that figure is now assessed at closer to one-fourth, or even higher. Most experts in the field of male eating disorders believe that the number has always been higher than reported."[27] According to Herrin, there are differences in how bulimia affects boys and men versus girls and women. Males, she says, are less concerned about strict weight control and are less likely to use purging to compensate for binge eating. Rather, their tendency is to use nonpurging methods such as excessive exercise.

In her book Herrin tells the story of a teenage boy named Travis, who was well liked by his friends, admired for his talent on the baseball diamond—and the last person anyone would suspect of having an eating disorder. So the first few times his friends found him in the bathroom throwing up, they assumed he had the stomach flu or had eaten something that did not agree with him. Herrin writes:

> But after enough of these episodes, they finally put two and two together and came to the undeniable conclusion that Travis had an eating disorder. Bulimia was the last

thing anyone thought he would struggle with, yet here he was suffering from a case so severe that eventually he was regularly noticing blood in his vomit. When Travis's friends finally approached him with their concerns, he himself had become frightened and desperately wanted to quit. The intervention of his friends was the push he needed; he was ready to take their advice and confide in his parents.[28]

Atypical Bulimics

Just as bulimia is considered a female condition, it is also typically perceived as a disorder of the young. John Prescott, who developed bulimia when he was nearly fifty years old, defies both stereotypes. The United Kingdom's former deputy prime minister, Prescott publicly announced in 2008 that he had struggled with bulimia for two decades. He kept the problem to himself as long as he did primarily out of shame and embarrassment, and also because of the stigma attached to the disorder. "It's such a strange thing for someone like me to confess to," he says. "People normally associate it with young women—anorexic girls, models trying to keep their weight down, or women in stressful situations, like Princess Diana." When he gorged on food, Prescott craved sweets, often consuming an entire can of Carnation sweetened condensed milk. He also binged when he would visit his favorite Chinese restaurant for dinner. "I could eat my way through the entire menu,"[29] he explains.

> Increasing numbers of middle-aged women are also admitting that they suffer from eating disorders such as bulimia.

Increasing numbers of middle-aged women are also admitting that they suffer from eating disorders such as bulimia. Anne E. Becker, a psychiatrist and researcher with Harvard Medical School, points out that "as our society values youth and as baby boomers reinvent what it means to be middle-aged, there are growing social forces that can undermine older women's self-esteem and potentially lead to body dissatisfaction."

The aging of eating disorder sufferers is reflected in the changes seen by treatment facilities such as the Renfrew Center, a facility with locations throughout the eastern and southeastern United States. Over the past decade, the number of Renfrew patients over the age of thirty-five has jumped 42 percent. The same is true of Denver's Eating Recovery Center, where several years ago an estimated 10 percent of patients were over twenty-five. Today 46 percent of the facility's patients are aged thirty and over.

A British woman named Heather Cooper has struggled with bulimia for more than fifteen years. She works as a sales and training manager, and although on the outside she appears to be polished and professional, on the inside she is in turmoil. Cooper knows that her binge eating and purging are harmful for her health, and she also knows she should stop—which she has been unable to do. "I am so embarrassed about my condition," she says. "I'm 45 and this is an illness linked to teenagers. But it has become a way of life for me. I will be in meetings and have to excuse myself to go to the toilet and be sick. I walk back in smiling. Yet inside I am in turmoil and spend my nights crying at home after binge-eating and then vomiting."[31]

The Loss of Control

Unlike many diseases and disorders that trace back to ancient times, bulimia did not capture the attention of scientists until 1979. Although it tends to be most common among young women, it affects males and females of all ages and all walks of life. Because of the powerful hold it has on sufferers, bulimia has been compared with an addiction to drugs. Says eating disorder specialist Anne White, "Bulimia is a way of controlling your emotions, so what starts as a crisis of body image becomes something darker that dominates your thinking."[32]

Primary Source Quotes*

What Is Bulimia?

66 Bulimia nervosa is often not diagnosed for many months or even years after onset because of the patients' secretiveness about their difficulties, usually associated with a great deal of shame. 99

—Christine Osterhout, "Bulimia Nervosa Clinical Presentation," Medscape, November 15, 2011.
http://emedicine.medscape.com.

Osterhout is a psychiatrist with the University of California, Davis, Health System.

66 Through purging, fasting, and exercise, bulimics hope to regain a sense of control they lacked while bingeing, but unfortunately they end up suffering such hunger that their cravings for food will take hold once again, making binge eating more likely. 99

—Princeton University Health Services, "Eating Disorders," April 18, 2012. www.princeton.edu.

Princeton University Health Services is a medical facility that provides comprehensive health care to university students and their dependents as well as to faculty and staff.

* Editor's Note: While the definition of a primary source can be narrowly or broadly defined, for the purposes of Compact Research, a primary source consists of: 1) results of original research presented by an organization or researcher; 2) eyewitness accounts of events, personal experience, or work experience; 3) first-person editorials offering pundits' opinions; 4) government officials presenting political plans and/or policies; 5) representatives of organizations presenting testimony or policy.

❝Unlike anorexia nervosa, bulimia nervosa patients are typically within normal weight range and restrict their total caloric consumption between binges.❞

—Kathleen N. Franco, "Eating Disorders," Cleveland Clinic, March 2012. www.clevelandclinicmeded.com.

Franco is a psychiatrist with the Cleveland Clinic.

❝Most individuals with bulimia are ashamed and secretive, sometimes going to great lengths to maintain the appearance of normal eating around other people.❞

—Lindsey Hall and Leigh Cohn, *Bulimia: A Guide to Recovery*. Carlsbad, CA: Gürze, 2011, pp. 26–27.

In 1980 Hall and Cohn wrote the first book on bulimia, which was based on Hall's struggle with the eating disorder and subsequent recovery from it.

❝Bulimia shares some features with anorexia; these people alternate between a careful restriction of eating and an almost complete loss of self-control.❞

—Gary L. Wenk, "The Connection Between Anorexia, Bulimia, and Marijuana," *Your Brain on Food* (blog), April 9, 2012. www.psychologytoday.com.

Wenk is a professor of psychology at Ohio State University and the author of *Your Brain on Food*.

❝Parents, teachers, coaches, or instructors may be able to identify the child or adolescent with bulimia, although many persons with the disorder initially keep their illness very private and hidden.❞

—Lucile Packard Children's Hospital at Stanford, "Child and Adolescent Bulimia Nervosa," 2012. www.lpch.org.

Lucile Packard Children's Hospital is an academic medical center on the campus of Stanford University.

❝A person with bulimia feels he or she cannot control the amount of food eaten.❞

—Office on Women's Health, "Bulimia Nervosa," March 29, 2010. www.womenshealth.gov.

The Office on Women's Health is an agency of the US Department of Health and Human Services.

❝People with bulimia . . . often fear gaining weight, want desperately to lose weight, and are intensely unhappy with their body size and shape.❞

—National Association of Anorexia Nervosa and Associated Disorders (ANAD), "Get Information: Bulimia Nervosa," 2012. www.anad.org.

The ANAD is a nonprofit organization that seeks to prevent and alleviate the problems of eating disorders.

❝Sometimes a person with anorexia or bulimia starts out just trying to lose some weight or hoping to get in shape. But the urge to eat less or to purge or over-exercise gets 'addictive' and becomes too hard to stop.❞

—Helen DeVos Children's Hospital, "Eating Disorders," January 2011. www.helendevoschildrens.org.

Located in Grand Rapids, Michigan, the Helen DeVos Children's Hospital is dedicated to improving the lives of children and their families.

What Is Bulimia?

- According to psychiatrist Roxanne Dryden-Edwards, the prevalence of bulimia among people in the United States has **doubled** since the 1960s.

- The International Association of Eating Disorders Professionals states that bulimia affects **1 to 2 percent** of adolescent and young adult females.

- According to the National Eating Disorders Association, **1 million** males in the United States suffer from either anorexia or bulimia.

- In a 2011 study of sixteen thousand children by Taiwanese researchers, **15 percent** of thirteen- to fifteen-year-olds and nearly **16 percent** of ten- to twelve-year-olds said they had tried vomiting to lose weight in the past year.

- A 2011 study published in the *Journal of Adolescent Health* found that teens from various racial backgrounds, including **Asian Americans and Latinos**, practiced extreme food-related behaviors, such as vomiting and laxative abuse, two to ten times more often than white teens.

- According to the South Carolina Department of Mental Health, **74 percent** of Native American girls use purging and/or diet pills as a way to lose weight.

Purging Most Common Among Hispanic Teens

Bulimia is characterized by cycles of overeating (bingeing) following by purging, which usually involves self-induced vomiting or taking laxatives in an attempt to rid the body of calories. According to a report published in July 2012 by the Child Trends Data Bank, purging behaviors are most common among Hispanic teens, followed by Caucasian and African American teens.

Percent of students in grades 9 to 12 who took laxatives or vomited to lose weight or avoid gaining weight during 2011

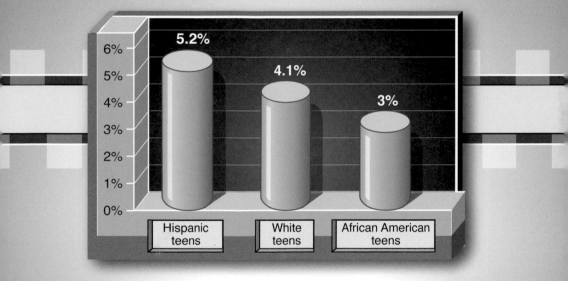

Source: Child Trends Data Bank, *Disordered Eating: Symptoms of Bulimia*, July 2012. www.childtrendsdatabank.org.

- The Eating Recovery Center in Denver, Colorado, states that **46 percent** of its patients are over thirty years of age.

- According to the National Eating Disorders Association, at any given time an estimated **5 percent** of the US population has undiagnosed bulimia.

Red Flags of Bulimia

Unlike anorexics, who are typically emaciated, people who suffer from bulimia are of normal weight, or slightly overweight. Thus, family members may not recognize the presence of an eating disorder. Over time, however, some or all of the symptoms will become apparent.

Obsessive preoccupation with body shape and weight; having a distorted, excessively negative body image
Living in fear of gaining weight; constantly worrying or complaining about being fat
Repeatedly eating unusually large quantities of food in one sitting, especially high-fat or sweet foods
Reluctance to eat in public or in front of others
Going to the bathroom immediately after eating or during meals
Exercising excessively
Sores, scars, or calluses on the knuckles or hands (from repeated self-induced vomiting)
Noticeably damaged teeth and gums

Source: Mayo Clinic, "Bulimia Nervosa," April 3, 2012. www.mayoclinic.com.

- The adolescent eating disorder facility Center for Discovery states that only **10 percent** of all eating disorder sufferers are males.

- According to the National Association of Anorexia Nervosa and Associated Disorders, people with bulimia often have coexisting psychological illnesses such as **depression, anxiety**, and/or **substance abuse** problems.

Bulimia Rare Among Males in South Korea

Studies have consistently shown that bulimia is much more common among females than males. In the United States, for example, bulimia affects girls and women at about three times the rate of boys and men—and the disparity is even more pronounced in South Korea. A study by the Korean national insurance service found that bulimia is nineteen times more common in females.

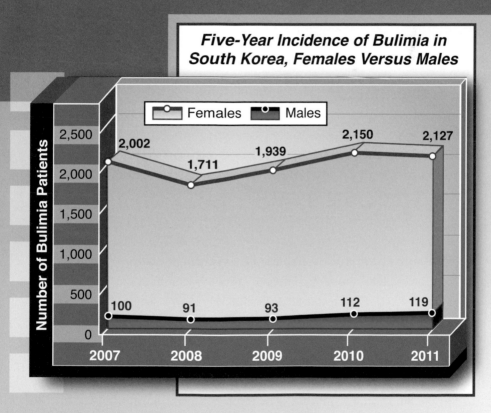

Five-Year Incidence of Bulimia in South Korea, Females Versus Males

Source: Lee Woo-Young, "Bulimia 19 Times More Common in Women than Men, . . . Survey Finds," *Korea Herald*, April 1, 2012. http://view.koreaherald.com.

- According to Oxford University psychiatrist John Powell, symptoms of bulimia affect up to **8 percent** of women in the United Kingdom.

- The Ohio State University Wexner Medical Center states that all **Western industrialized countries** have reported the incidence of bulimia.

What Causes Bulimia?

> **❝There is no simple answer to the question of what causes bulimia.❞**
>
> —National Health Service, the United Kingdom's health care system.

> **❝Factors believed to contribute to the development of bulimia include cultural ideals and social attitudes toward body appearance.❞**
>
> —Lucile Packard Children's Hospital at Stanford, an academic medical center on the campus of Stanford University.

Scientists have studied bulimia for over thirty years and have learned a great deal about it. Through their research, most have become convinced that bulimia does not have one single cause. Rather, multiple causes are likely involved, such as genetics, personality traits, emotions, stress, and environmental factors, among others. Although the dynamics are not well understood, some or all of these likely factors work together in the development of bulimia.

One emotional issue that is extremely common among people with bulimia is a deep fear of being fat. The fear can be so overwhelming that they are willing to resort to drastic measures in order to keep from gaining weight. This was the case with a Columbus, Ohio, woman named Paula. As a teenager she was what she calls "plus size,"[33] and she was driven to lose weight because of a circumstance that few people knew about: She was the sole caregiver for a mother who weighed more than 600 pounds (272kg). "Day-in and day-out," says Paula, "I watched my mother slip away from life, functionally and mentally. All over food. Or so I thought at the time. Secretly resentful, I was determined to never get 'that big.'"[34] Consumed by her fear of becoming obese, Paula resorted to bingeing and purging in a desperate attempt to keep that from happening.

Bulimic Athletes

Competitive athletes and dancers have an especially high risk of developing bulimia, largely because they are under constant pressure to keep their weight down. According to psychotherapist and eating disorder specialist Stephen M. Mathis, the adolescent male athletes who most often develop bulimia are those who participate in wrestling, boxing, and body building. Yet the problem often goes unrecognized. "Since athletes are frequently reinforced for maintaining and/or 'making weight,'" says Mathis, "eating disordered behaviors often go undiagnosed by coaches or parents as being a 'normal' part of the process and sacrifice needed with serious competitors."[35] Studies have shown that wrestlers keep their body fat levels as low as 3 percent, which is far below what is considered healthy. According to the National Eating Disorders Association, competitive wrestlers have been known to drop weight rapidly by using a combination of food restriction and ridding their bodies of excess fluid by using laxatives, diuretics, and other purging methods.

Former athletes are also at risk for developing bulimia. Once they are no longer involved in their sport, many lose their sense of identity and become obsessed with eating and weight loss. This was the case with Alyssa Kitasoe, who was a star gymnast for the University of California, Los Angeles. Kitasoe had been involved in gymnastics since she was seven years old but had to give it up in college. At that point she slowly began to gain weight, which was very disturbing to her, as she explains: "You still have the mind-set that you need to be tiny. You compare yourself to the way you were."[36] Kitasoe says she thought about food constantly but starved herself throughout the day. By the time evening arrived she was famished and often gorged on food, at times eating

> " One emotional issue that is extremely common among people with bulimia is a deep fear of being fat. "

an entire pizza and a large bag of chips. Then, consumed with guilt, she would force herself to vomit.

The Futile Quest for Perfection

Research has consistently shown that personality traits such as perfectionism are a risk factor for developing bulimia. People who are perfectionists have unrealistically high expectations for themselves and are often convinced that they can never be attractive enough or thin enough. To examine the connection between perfectionist traits and eating disorders, a group of researchers from Belgium conducted a study that was published in 2011. The team, which was led by psychologist Liesbet Boone, followed the behavior of 559 adolescents over a period of two years and evaluated two types of perfectionist traits: personal standard (PS) perfectionism, which involves setting high standards and expectations for oneself; and evaluative concerns (EC) perfectionism, meaning the tendency to be hypercritical of one's own behavior and performance as well as intolerant of mistakes. The team concluded that EC perfectionism was the most significant risk factor for the development of bulimia. As Boone explains, "This finding suggests that being overly critical of one's own behavior and performance increases the risk to experience bulimic symptoms two years later."[37]

> " Research has consistently shown that personality traits such as perfectionism are a risk factor for developing bulimia. "

Allison Kreiger Walsh is an example of someone who became bulimic as a direct result of her extreme perfectionism. A former Miss Florida, Walsh grew up in a very competitive home with a mother who had been a national champion baton twirler. As far back as she can remember, Walsh was determined to settle for nothing less than perfection in everything she did, from academics to athletics. "I was a complete perfectionist and put a lot of pressure on myself," she says. "From pushing myself in the gym to expecting straight As on my report card, I didn't want to settle for anything less than the best."[38]

Like her mother, Walsh became a champion baton twirler as well as a dancer. She had many friends and was extremely popular in school—but her life began to unravel after she developed bulimia. By the time she was a senior in high school, Walsh was caught in the throes of the disorder, forcing herself to vomit as often as twelve times a day. Her symptoms were obvious to everyone around her, and her health was deteriorating rapidly. "I was extremely weak," she says, "I had lost half the hair on my head, I had broken blood vessels in my eyes, I had done damage to my esophagus from the bingeing and purging, I couldn't digest food properly even if I wanted to, and I was at a dangerously low weight."[39] By November of that year Walsh acknowledged that she had a terribly serious problem. She knew she could not go on that way any longer and told her parents that she needed help.

Genetic Connections

For many years mental health experts believed that eating disorders were caused solely by environmental influences, especially bad parenting. Although parents can have a strong influence on children's behavior, including whether they develop eating disorders, it is now known that genetics can also play a role. As psychologists and eating disorder experts Suzanne E. Mazzeo and Cynthia M. Bulik explain: "The significant role genetic factors play in the development of eating disorders is becoming increasingly clear."[40] According to Mazzeo and Bulik, family studies have consistently found a higher lifetime prevalence of bulimia or anorexia in people whose close relatives also suffer from eating disorders.

The genetic aspect of eating disorders was the focus of a 2010 study of twins that was conducted by researchers from Michigan State University (MSU) and Florida State University. Specifically, the team wanted to determine the role that genetics might play in the development of eating disorders during adolescence. Led by MSU psychologist Kelly Klump, the researchers studied 198 sets of female twins aged ten to fifteen who were going through puberty. Klump's

> " Although parents can have a strong influence on children's behavior, including whether they develop eating disorders, it is now known that genetics can also play a role. "

> Studies have shown that among adolescents with eating disorders, it is common for one or both parents to be preoccupied with their own bodies and appearance, be obsessed with exercise, and/or have unhealthy eating behaviors themselves.

team found that the influence of genes was much greater in pubertal girls who had particularly high levels of estradiol, a form of the hormone estrogen that is responsible for growth of female reproductive organs.

Although the researchers could not determine exactly which genes were being influenced by estradiol, Klump says knowing that the hormone is involved in the development of eating disorders is an important discovery. She explains: "The reason we see an increase in genetic influences during puberty is that the genes for disordered eating are essentially getting switched on during that time. This research was trying to figure out why. What's turning on the genes during puberty? And what we found is that increases in estradiol apparently are activating genetic risk for eating disorders."[41] Klump adds that additional research is needed to further explore these findings and to identify specific genes that might be influenced by estradiol.

"Complex Traits"

As significant as genetics are in the development of bulimia or anorexia, environmental factors also play a role. Genetics alone cannot be responsible because many (even most) people who are biologically predisposed do not develop the disorder. "By definition," Mazzeo and Bulik explain, "eating disorders are complex traits. That means . . . they are influenced by multiple genetic and environmental factors of small to moderate effect. There is not one gene for anorexia nervosa or one gene for bulimia nervosa."[42] Numerous scientists share the perspective that genetics and environmental factors work together to cause bulimia. To illustrate that concept, mental health professionals often use the metaphor of biology loading a gun and environment pulling the trigger.

The complex combination of genetics and environment means that a child's interaction with parents becomes especially important. If, for example, someone is genetically vulnerable and his or her parents overemphasize the ideal body shape and thinness, the person's risk for developing anorexia or bulimia is markedly higher. Studies have shown that among adolescents with eating disorders, it is common for one or both parents to be preoccupied with their own bodies and appearance, be obsessed with exercise, and/or have unhealthy eating behaviors themselves. Mazzeo and Bulik write:

> Mothers' comments about their own weight and appearance are associated with the body esteem of their fourth and fifth grade daughters and sons, and mothers who complain about their own weight are more likely to have daughters who are weight concerned. . . . Thus, although not solely causal, the principle of children being more likely to "do as you do" rather than "do as you say" renders parental role modeling of healthy eating and weight behaviors important to the task of creating a protective environment—especially in genetically vulnerable offspring.[43]

Society and the Media

Many eating disorder specialists are convinced that the value society places on thinness and the media's glorification of this ideal play a significant role in the development of bulimia. Proponents of that point of view stress that the eating disorder was virtually unknown before the 1960s; since then the number of bulimia cases has soared. Over that same period of time, media penetration—and influence—have steadily grown, most notably with the rapid growth of the Internet since the introduction of the World Wide Web in the early 1990s. So, more than ever before, people are exposed to prolific images of skinny, beautiful people on television and in movies, on the pages of magazines, and on the Internet.

Psychiatrist Anne E. Becker, who is a researcher with Harvard Medical School, has been studying the connection between media influence and eating disorders for several decades, and her focus has been on the Pacific island country of Fiji. When she visited Fiji in 1995, she was struck by how much enjoyment the Fijian people got from eating good food, as well as how their culture valued larger, curvaceous bodies in females. At that time, people who lived in Fiji did not have televisions, and eating disorders were nonexistent. But when Becker returned to the country just three years later, she was stunned at the difference. Western culture had infiltrated the country with the arrival of television, and the effect this was having on young girls was striking. According to Becker, Fijian girls told her that they wanted to look like the skinny females they saw on television. Because they no longer liked their bodies, more than 11 percent reported that they had purged in an effort to lose weight.

Today television is found in about 85 percent of Fijian homes in cities and towns, and about 8 percent of homes in rural areas. For a study that was published in June 2010, Becker made a number of interesting discoveries. She found that the risk of eating disorders was not dependent on whether girls had direct exposure to television in their own homes. Their association with peers who had been exposed to television was shown to be a more powerful factor than actually watching the programs themselves. After extensive interviews with adolescent girls, Becker found that higher exposure to media content through contact with peers was linked to a 60 percent increase in a girl's chances of developing an eating disorder such as bulimia. "Our study showed the strength of social network exposure to the risk for eating disorder symptoms," says Becker, "and it is particularly concerning to see a small scale indigent population undergoing a rapid social change when exposed to a western-produced risk. It's a new hazard to their social environment."[44]

A Perplexing Condition

As much as scientists have learned about bulimia, they still have many questions about why it develops. A number of contributing factors have been identified, including genetics, personality traits, and emotional issues, as well as environmental factors such as society's attitude about beauty and thinness. These are believed to work together in complex ways, but exactly how that happens remains a mystery.

What Causes Bulimia?

66 As with most mental illnesses, eating disorders are not caused by just one factor but by a combination of sociocultural, psychological and biological factors. 99

—Mental Health America, "Eating Disorders," 2012. www.nmha.org.

Mental Health America is dedicated to helping all people live mentally healthier lives and educating the public about mental health and mental illness.

66 It is already widely accepted that there is a genetic component to bulimia, the exact nature of which is still unknown. 99

—Lindsey Hall and Leigh Cohn, *Bulimia: A Guide to Recovery*. Carlsbad, CA: Gürze, 2011, p. 35.

In 1980 Hall and Cohn wrote the first book on bulimia, which was based on Hall's struggle with the eating disorder and subsequent recovery from it.

66 Dieting can start the course of bulimia. 99

—Linda Mintle, "Bulimia: Shame the Silencer." *Weight & Body* (blog), March 21, 2011. http://drlindamintle.com.

Mintle is a licensed marriage and family therapist.

* Editor's Note: While the definition of a primary source can be narrowly or broadly defined, for the purposes of Compact Research, a primary source consists of: 1) results of original research presented by an organization or researcher; 2) eyewitness accounts of events, personal experience, or work experience; 3) first-person editorials offering pundits' opinions; 4) government officials presenting political plans and/or policies; 5) representatives of organizations presenting testimony or policy.

"Anorexia and bulimia may be due to an imbalance in brain chemistry."

—Gary L. Wenk, "The Connection Between Anorexia, Bulimia, and Marijuana," *Your Brain on Food* (blog), April 9, 2012. www.psychologytoday.com.

Wenk is a professor of psychology at Ohio State University and the author of *Your Brain on Food*.

"It is very likely that the commonly cited figure of one million males with eating disorders in the United States will soon become an out-dated figure for a much higher number."

—National Association for Males with Eating Disorders, "Statistics: Research," 2011. www.namedinc.org.

The National Association for Males with Eating Disorders provides support to males with eating disorders and serves as a resource of information for the public.

"Families of patients with bulimia nervosa have higher rates of substance abuse, particularly alcoholism, affective disorders, and obesity."

—Kathleen N. Franco, "Eating Disorders," Cleveland Clinic, March 2012. www.clevelandclinicmeded.com.

Franco is a psychiatrist with the Cleveland Clinic.

"There is some evidence that women who have a sister or mother with bulimia are at higher risk of developing the condition."

—University of Maryland Medical Center, "Bulimia Nervosa," September 11, 2010. www.umm.edu.

The University of Maryland Medical Center is in partnership with the University of Maryland School of Medicine in Baltimore.

66 Bulimia . . . can stem from family problems, traumatic experiences, or insecurities. **99**

—April Uffner, "The Vicious Cycle of Bulimia," Yahoo! Voices, July 2, 2012. http://voices.yahoo.com.

Uffner is a young woman who struggled with bulimia throughout her high school and college years.

66 Athletes and dancers are particularly vulnerable to developing eating disorders around the time of puberty, as they may want to stop or suppress growth (both height and weight). **99**

—Helen DeVos Children's Hospital, "Eating Disorders," January, 2011. www.helendevoschildrens.org.

Located in Grand Rapids, Michigan, the Helen DeVos Children's Hospital is dedicated to improving the lives of children and their families.

Facts and Illustrations

What Causes Bulimia?

- According to the Eating Disorders Coalition for Research, Policy, and Action, the risk of developing an eating disorder is **50 to 80 percent** determined by genetics.

- For a study published in 2011, researchers from Belgium evaluated 559 adolescents for two years and found that **perfectionism** was the most significant risk factor for eating disorders, especially bulimia.

- According to Britain's National Health Service, people who have a **close relative** with bulimia are four times more likely to develop it than those who do not have a relative with the disorder.

- In a 2011 Harvard Medical School study in Fiji, researchers found that having peers who had high media exposure was linked to a **60 percent** increase in a girl's chances of developing an eating disorder.

- According to physician Christine Osterhout, bulimia is a higher risk for those whose occupation or hobbies require gaining and/or losing weight rapidly, such as **wrestlers** and competitive **bodybuilders**.

- A 2011 study by researchers from Taiwan involved sixteen thousand school-age children trying to lose weight. It found that among those who intentionally made themselves vomit, using a computer for more than two hours a day increased the vomiting risk by **55 percent**, eating fried food every day by **110 percent**, and having nighttime snacks every day by **51 percent**.

Triggered by Dieting

Scientists believe that a number of contributing factors work together in the development of bulimia. For many people the disorder is rooted in a negative, distorted body image, which compels them to lose weight. Strict dieting leads to overwhelming cravings, which in turn lead to bingeing and purging—and before long sufferers are caught in a destructive cycle from which they cannot escape.

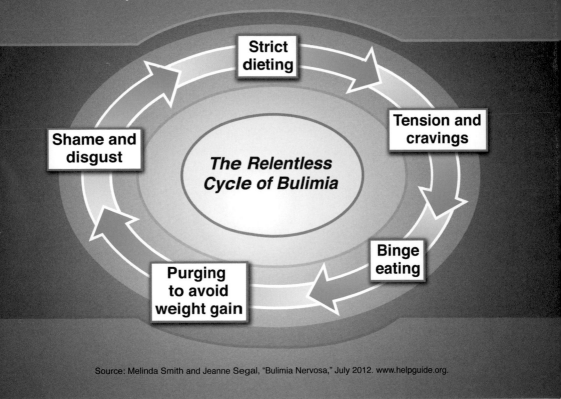

Source: Melinda Smith and Jeanne Segal, "Bulimia Nervosa," July 2012. www.helpguide.org.

- According to the Kartini Clinic for Disordered Eating, bulimia in females is about **five times as common** as anorexia.

- The National Women's Health Information Center states that traumatic incidents such as **abuse or rape** can lead to the onset of an eating disorder.

Coexistence of Bulimia and Other Disorders

Although scientists cannot cite one specific cause for bulimia, they have identified a number of contributing factors, such as psychological and emotional problems. Examining the coexistence of eating disorders and other mental illnesses was one of the focuses of a study published in March 2011 by researchers from the United States and France. As this graph shows, the researchers found that a high percentage of adolescents with bulimia also suffered from other mental disorders.

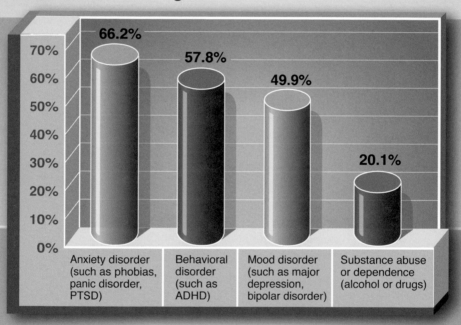

Adolescents with eating disorders and other mental disorders

Source: Sonja A. Swanson et al. "Prevalence and Correlates of Eating Disorders in Adolescents," PubMed.gov, March 7, 2011. www.ncbi.nlm.nih.gov.

- In a February 2010 survey by the Girl Scouts of America, **47 percent** of teen girl respondents said that fashion magazines gave them a body image to strive for.

Facebook Negatively Affects Body Image

For many years eating disorder specialists have warned that media glamorization of skinny bodies can have a profound impact on young people's self-image and possibly play a role in the development of eating disorders. Today, media have more influence than ever because of the soaring popularity of social networking sites such as Facebook. A February 2012 survey of 600 Facebook users aged 16 to 40 found that many people (especially women) are not happy with their bodies, and their participation in Facebook is fueling that negativity—and leading to harmful behaviors.

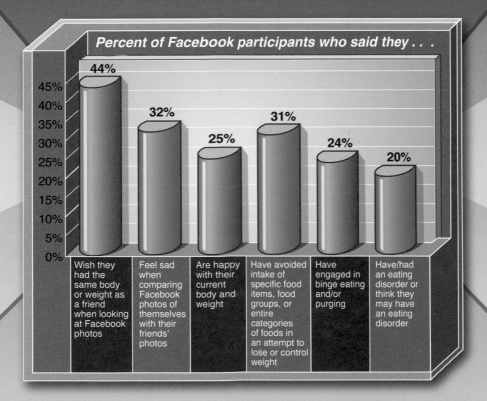

Percent of Facebook participants who said they . . .

44%	Wish they had the same body or weight as a friend when looking at Facebook photos
32%	Feel sad when comparing Facebook photos of themselves with their friends' photos
25%	Are happy with their current body and weight
31%	Have avoided intake of specific food items, food groups, or entire categories of foods in an attempt to lose or control weight
24%	Have engaged in binge eating and/or purging
20%	Have/had an eating disorder or think they may have an eating disorder

Source: Kathleen Shaffer, "Public Survey Conducted by the Center for Eating Disorders at Sheppard Pratt Finds Facebook Use Impacts the Way Many People Feel About Their Bodies," Center for Eating Disorders at Sheppard Pratt, March 28, 2012. http://eatingdisorder.org.

- According to physician David B. Merrill, researchers have identified specific **chromosomes** that may be associated with bulimia and anorexia.

What Are the
Risks of Bulimia?

66Bulimia can be dangerous. It may lead to serious medical complications over time.99

—National Institutes of Health, the largest medical research agency in the United States.

66Bulimia, and the medical problems that result, can damage nearly every organ system in the body, and may be fatal.99

—Children's Hospital Boston, a comprehensive pediatric health care facility located in Boston, Massachusetts.

Bulimia can take a devastating toll on a person's health. Repeated self-induced vomiting can cause everything from destruction of tooth enamel and sores in the mouth to a ruptured esophagus, which is the tube that carries food, liquids, and saliva from the mouth to the stomach. Both vomiting and abuse of laxatives can lead to chronic constipation, as well as to internal bleeding and severe damage to the kidneys, bowel, and liver. Yet despite knowing the risks, many with bulimia are unable to stop the bingeing and purging cycle, as a sufferer named Christina writes:

> Bulimia is just like any other compulsion, you think you are the one in control when the opposite is true, the compulsion or addiction is in control of you. . . . Many times I've worried that my heart is just going to stop or one of these days my esophagus is going to rupture when I'm purging, which can happen. How can I know that what I'm doing can lead to death and keep doing it?[45]

Deadly Disruption

The fears expressed by Christina are not unfounded, including the reference to her heart stopping. Heart problems are a significant risk of bulimia because recurrent purging can lead to a dangerous imbalance in electrolytes, which play an essential role in the body's ability to function properly. Electrolytes are so named because they trigger electrical impulses in the body that enable cells to communicate with each other. This, in turn, allows muscles and nerves to function, moves water and fluids (blood and plasma) throughout the body, maintains heart rate and blood pressure, and facilitates the rebuilding of damaged tissue.

Electrolyte levels are kept in proper balance by a variety of hormones that are produced by the kidneys, adrenal glands (atop the kidneys), and pituitary gland. Physician Benjamin Wedro explains:

> Sensors in specialized kidney cells monitor the amount of sodium, potassium, and water in the bloodstream. The body functions in a very narrow range of normal, and it is hormones like renin (made in the kidney), angiotensin (from the lung, brain and heart), aldosterone (from the adrenal gland), and antidiuretic hormone (from the pituitary) that keep the electrolyte balance within those normal limits.[46]

It is normal for people to lose electrolytes when their bodies lose moisture, such as through sweating. But when someone becomes dehydrated from repeated vomiting or from abuse of laxatives or diuretics, electrolytes can be quickly thrown out of balance—which creates a dangerous situation. Early symptoms of electrolyte imbalance include low blood pressure and irregular heart rate, which can quickly progress to permanent heart damage, cardiac arrest (heart attack), and death.

In October 2009 twenty-one-year-old Ben Spencer died from a heart attack that was caused by complications of bulimia. Spencer had struggled with the disorder since he was a teenager. He had been bullied in high school because of his weight, so he began to exercise at least five hours each day. Afterward he gorged on pizza, fried foods, and sugary snacks and then forced himself to vomit. At one point he lost so much weight that staff members at a gym banned him from the facility, but he just found another place to exercise. Although his family suspected that he had an eating disorder, Spencer continued to deny it and attempted to hide his emaciated body by wearing baggy track suits. Three weeks before his death, Spencer's girlfriend had a baby girl. His mother, Michaela Richen, recalls that "Ben had just become a dad and he was trying to get better but it had just gone too far—no one could help him anymore."[47]

Fertility and Pregnancy Risks

Repeated bingeing and purging can cause hormonal changes that interfere with a woman's ability to ovulate, which can lead to irregular menstrual cycles or stop menstruation altogether. According to the American Pregnancy Association, an estimated 50 percent of women with bulimia do not have regular periods, and this can make it difficult for them to get pregnant—or make pregnancy impossible. This was the case with British actress Chantelle Houghton. In July 2011 she publicly announced that doctors had told her she would never be able to conceive naturally because of her long-running difficulties with bulimia. Houghton has struggled with the disorder since she was fourteen years old, and keeping her weight down has always been a difficult battle for her.

When she was at her thinnest, Houghton was vomiting on a regular basis. "I was making myself sick a lot," she says. "Food was just coming straight back out of me. I was obsessed from the minute I woke up in the morning until the minute I went to bed. I was constantly watching what I was eating." Now, Houghton is painfully aware of the steep price she has paid for her obsession with being thin, and for all the years of purging. She explains: "I've punished my body, and now it's punishing me. Ultimately it's my fault. I hate myself and can never forgive myself." Houghton wants other women to know about her experience and understand the devastating toll that bulimia can take on their health and their fertility. "I hope they'll see what's happened to me and realise what they're doing—the long-term effects," she says. "I'm 27 and I can't have children naturally. Being stick-thin—is it worth that?"[48]

> "Bulimia can take a devastating toll on a person's health."

Not all bulimia sufferers are left infertile because of their disorder—but if they do become pregnant, continued bingeing and purging can cause a number of serious problems. The growing fetus receives all its nourishment from the mother's body. According to the National Eating Disorders Association, when stores of carbohydrates, proteins, fats, vitamins, minerals, and other nutrients are low, a woman's body will drain them to support the fetus's growth and development. The group writes: "If reserves are not sufficiently restored through healthy eating, the mother can become severely malnourished, and this in turn can lead to depression, exhaustion and many other serious health complications." The NEDA goes on to describe how pregnancy raises the risks already faced by women with bulimia: "Women with bulimia nervosa who continue to purge may suffer dehydration, chemical imbalances or even cardiac irregularities. Pregnancy heightens these health risks."[49]

> **When someone becomes dehydrated from repeated vomiting or from abuse of laxatives or diuretics, electrolytes can be quickly thrown out of balance—which creates a dangerous situation.**

If the mother continues to binge and purge while she is pregnant, she is putting her baby at risk. As the Office on Women's Health explains, "If a woman takes laxatives or diuretics during pregnancy, her baby could be harmed. These things take away nutrients and fluids from a woman before they are able to feed and nourish the baby."[50] Possible difficulties include miscarriage, complications during labor and delivery, increased risk of cesarean birth, premature birth, low birth weight, and birth defects, such as blindness or mental retardation. Among the most serious risks is preeclampsia, a dangerous medical condition that is characterized by a rapid rise in blood pressure. If a pregnant woman develops preeclampsia, she can have seizures, a stroke, and/or suffer from multiple organ failure and death. The condition can also result in the baby being stillborn.

Bulimia and Substance Abuse

Years of research have consistently shown that there is a strong association between eating disorders and alcohol and/or drug abuse. In a report published in 2010, New York psychologist Lisa R. Cohen and colleagues discussed this association and recapped the collective findings of a number of previous studies. In reference to a national study of more than ten thousand American adults, the report states that the lifetime co-occurrence of alcohol-use disorders and eating disorders ranged from 25 percent to 34 percent, and lifetime co-occurrence of drug use disorders and eating disorders ranged from 18 percent to 26 percent. The group writes: "These rates are much higher than those found in the general population."[51]

Also based on their analysis, the researchers concluded that people with bulimia had a greater risk for developing substance abuse than those who suffer from anorexia. They cited a population-based study finding that 22.9 percent of bulimic women suffered from alcohol dependence, and nearly 50 percent regularly abused alcohol. Citing information from a previous study, the 2010 report states that "by the age of 35, 50% of individuals with bulimia nervosa had met criteria for alcohol abuse or dependence at some point in their lives. Though alcohol appears to be the most frequent substance of choice, other substances are also often abused by bulimic women including cocaine, amphetamines and other stimulants."[52]

> "Repeated bingeing and purging can cause hormonal changes that interfere with a woman's ability to ovulate, which can lead to irregular menstrual cycles or stop menstruation altogether.

Taylor Ellsworth can relate to this because she also struggled with alcohol and drug abuse when she was suffering from bulimia. Ellsworth developed the disorder when she was fourteen years old. At first she considered self-induced vomiting to be a "handy tool to un-do the moments where I lost the illusion of self-control." But over the next few years she began drinking heavily and realized that all the calories in alcohol were causing her to gain weight. So, her solution was to starve herself during the day and binge, purge and drink at night, which left her feeling physically and emotionally sick.

Ellsworth continued on this downward spiral throughout high school. In addition to bingeing, purging, and drinking, she began using drugs. Before graduating from high school, she was hospitalized for a week with a condition known as bradycardia, which is a slower-than-normal heart rate caused by the heart's not pumping enough oxygen-rich blood to the body. "I knew that I was close to death," she says. Ellsworth eventually overcame her alcohol addiction through participation in Alcoholics Anonymous, but says it took longer—and was much more difficult—to overcome bulimia. "The thing about an eating disorder," she says, "is that it's impossible to ever really be free from it: it can't be escaped the way drugs and alcohol can since living requires eating multiple times a day."[53]

Altering the Brain

Scientists have long been interested in how the bingeing and purging behaviors of bulimia affect the brain. Studies have shown that when the body is robbed of nutrients, brain function can be disrupted, affecting a sufferer's ability to concentrate and make decisions. Also, says the eating disorders treatment facility Recovery Ranch: "Those with bulimia sometimes suffer from psychological problems that can last for years and even endanger their lives. Some individuals fall into such great depression that they may become suicidal."[54]

Examining the effects of bulimia on the brain was the focus of a study published in October 2011 by researchers from Denver, Colorado. Based on previous studies with laboratory animals, the team sought to investigate the effects of bulimic behaviors on dopamine, which is a chemical that helps control the brain's reward and pleasure centers and regulates behaviors such as learning and motivation. By using magnetic resonance imaging

> " Years of research have consistently shown that there is a strong association between eating disorders and alcohol and/ or drug abuse. "

technology to scan the brains of healthy women and women with bulimia, the team found a distinct difference in brain activity among the two groups. When the women were given tasks designed to stimulate the production of dopamine, those with bulimia showed weakened brain response. This confirmed the theory that bulimic behavior can have noticeable effects on the brain. Lead researcher Guido Frank explains, "We found reduced activation in this network in the bulimic women, and the more often an individual had binge/purge episodes the less responsive was their brain. That suggests that the eating disorder behavior directly affects brain function."[55]

The List Goes On

People who suffer from bulimia can do immense damage to their health. Repeated bingeing and purging can alter the brain's ability to function properly, as well as throwing electrolytes out of balance, which could lead to death from a heart attack. Bulimic women can stop having periods and endanger their ability to conceive a child, and bingeing and purging during pregnancy puts the health of the mother and baby at risk. These and other severe health problems are unfortunate realities of bulimia that can only be avoided if sufferers can manage to break free from the downward spiral in which they are caught.

What Are the Risks of Bulimia?

66 A person with bulimia can be at high risk for death because of purging and its impact on the heart and electrolyte imbalances. Laxative use and excessive exercise can increase risk of death in individuals who are actively bulimic. 99

—National Eating Disorders Association, "Common Myths About Eating Disorders," *NEDA Toolkit for Coaches and Trainers*, August 2010. www.nationaleatingdisorders.org.

Through education, advocacy, and research, the National Eating Disorders Association seeks to expand public understanding of eating disorders, increase prevention efforts, and promote access to treatment.

66 The most common causes of sudden death in bulimia are cardiac or respiratory arrest, the result of electrolyte imbalances from excessive purging. 99

—Lindsey Hall and Leigh Cohn, *Bulimia: A Guide to Recovery*. Carlsbad, CA: Gürze, 2011, p. 50.

In 1980 Hall and Cohn wrote the first book on bulimia, which was based on Hall's struggle with the eating disorder and subsequent recovery from it.

Primary Source Quotes

* Editor's Note: While the definition of a primary source can be narrowly or broadly defined, for the purposes of Compact Research, a primary source consists of: 1) results of original research presented by an organization or researcher; 2) eyewitness accounts of events, personal experience, or work experience; 3) first-person editorials offering pundits' opinions; 4) government officials presenting political plans and/or policies; 5) representatives of organizations presenting testimony or policy.

> **"Death is a relatively uncommon outcome for bulimia."**

—Patricia Quigley, "Pediatric Bulimia," Medscape, December 20, 2011. http://emedicine.medscape.com.

Quigley is a pediatrician with the University of Wisconsin Hospital and Clinics.

....

> **"Binge eating can stretch out the stomach or even cause it to rupture. Excessive exercise weakens your immune system and can destroy your muscles. The list goes on and on."**

—Emily K. Sandoz, Kelly G. Wilson, and Troy DuFrene, *The Mindfulness & Acceptance Workbook for Bulimia: A Guide to Breaking Free from Bulimia.* Oakland, CA: New Harbinger, 2011, p. 19.

Sandoz is a professor of psychology at the University of Louisiana, Lafayette; Wilson is a psychologist from the University of Mississippi; and DuFrene is a writer from Oakland, California, who specializes in mental health issues.

....

> **"Bulimia can result in a sore throat, worn-away tooth enamel, acid reflux, and heart attacks."**

—American Psychological Association, "Eating Disorders," October 2011. www.apa.org.

The American Psychological Association is a scientific and professional organization that represents the field of psychology in the United States.

....

> **"Women who have stopped having periods because of bulimia will be unable to become pregnant."**

—University of Maryland Medical Center, "Bulimia Nervosa," September 11, 2010. www.umm.edu.

The University of Maryland Medical Center is in partnership with the University of Maryland School of Medicine in Baltimore.

....

❝Patients with bulimia often suffer from low self-esteem and depression.❞

—John Powell, "Bulimia Nervosa," NetDoctor, March 29, 2011. www.netdoctor.co.uk.

Powell, a psychiatry graduate from Oxford University, works in the field of public health medicine in Buckinghamshire, England.

❝The recurrent binge-and-purge cycles of bulimia can affect the entire digestive system and can lead to electrolyte and chemical imbalances in the body that affect the heart and other major organ functions.❞

—Jill Smith, "Dr. Smith Explains the Health Consequences of Bulimia Nervosa," *Health and Wellness* (blog), July 11, 2011. http://drjillsmithwellnessblog.com.

Smith is a Boston dentist who works closely with physicians, nutritionists, and mental health professionals to help people who suffer from bulimia.

What Are the Risks of Bulimia?

- According to Britain's National Health Service, excessive use of **laxatives** by someone with bulimia can damage the **bowel muscles**, resulting in **permanent constipation**.

- The Mayo Clinic states that one risk of bulimia is **dehydration**, which can lead to serious medical problems such as **kidney failure**.

- According to clinical psychologist Lavinia Rodriguez, medical complications that can accompany bulimia include **rupturing stomach**, **heart problems**, and an **inflamed esophagus**.

- The Eating Disorders Association estimates that **10 percent** of bulimics **will die** as a result of their disorder.

- New York psychotherapist Susan Schulherr says that as many as **50 percent** of young women with bulimia have **irregular menstrual periods**.

- A 2012 study by researchers from Drexel University found that the longer women battle bulimia, the more their **weight will climb**.

- The National Eating Disorders Association states that up to **89 percent** of bulimia patients show signs of tooth erosion caused by repeated vomiting.

Bulimia's Damaging Toll on the Body

The recurrent bingeing and purging that are characteristic of bulimia can be devastating to the body, causing everything from muscle fatigue and dry skin to organ damage and death.

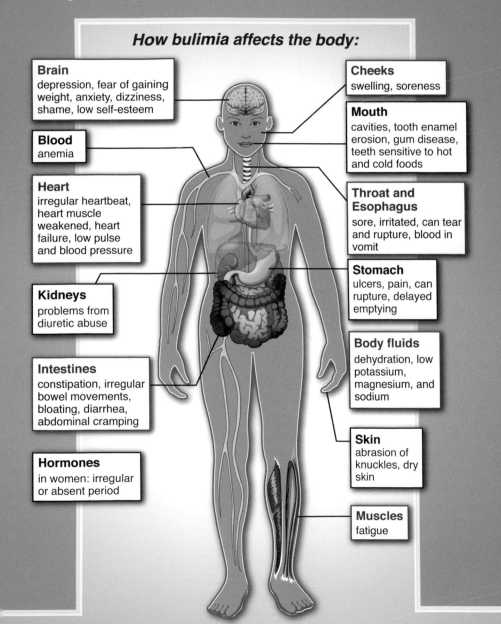

How bulimia affects the body:

Brain
depression, fear of gaining weight, anxiety, dizziness, shame, low self-esteem

Blood
anemia

Heart
irregular heartbeat, heart muscle weakened, heart failure, low pulse and blood pressure

Kidneys
problems from diuretic abuse

Intestines
constipation, irregular bowel movements, bloating, diarrhea, abdominal cramping

Hormones
in women: irregular or absent period

Cheeks
swelling, soreness

Mouth
cavities, tooth enamel erosion, gum disease, teeth sensitive to hot and cold foods

Throat and Esophagus
sore, irritated, can tear and rupture, blood in vomit

Stomach
ulcers, pain, can rupture, delayed emptying

Body fluids
dehydration, low potassium, magnesium, and sodium

Skin
abrasion of knuckles, dry skin

Muscles
fatigue

Source: Office on Women's Health, "Bulimia Nervosa," US Department of Health and Human Services, June 15, 2009. www.womenshealth.gov.

61

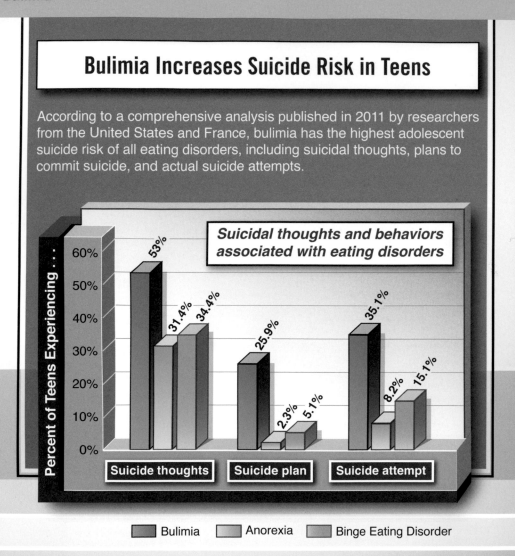

Bulimia Increases Suicide Risk in Teens

According to a comprehensive analysis published in 2011 by researchers from the United States and France, bulimia has the highest adolescent suicide risk of all eating disorders, including suicidal thoughts, plans to commit suicide, and actual suicide attempts.

Suicidal thoughts and behaviors associated with eating disorders

Percent of Teens Experiencing . . .

- Suicide thoughts: Bulimia 53%, Anorexia 31.4%, Binge Eating Disorder 34.4%
- Suicide plan: Bulimia 25.9%, Anorexia 2.3%, Binge Eating Disorder 5.1%
- Suicide attempt: Bulimia 35.1%, Anorexia 8.2%, Binge Eating Disorder 15.1%

Bulimia ■ Anorexia ■ Binge Eating Disorder

Source: Sonja A. Swanson et al. "Prevalence and Correlates of Eating Disorders in Adolescents," PubMed.gov, March 7, 2011. www.ncbi.nlm.nih.gov/pubmed.

- According to the National Institutes of Health, frequent vomiting by those who suffer from bulimia sends **stomach acid into the esophagus**, which can cause permanent damage.

- California specialist physician Melissa Conrad Stöppler states that **20 to 40 percent** of women with bulimia also suffer from problems having to do with drug or alcohol use.

Bulimia and Anorexia Can Lead to Fertility Problems

One of the risks of bulimia and anorexia for women who are of childbearing age is that the disorder can interfere with ovulation and menstrual cycles. This, in turn, affects their ability to conceive. A 2011 study of over 11,000 women by researchers from King's College London found that women who suffered from both anorexia and bulimia took longer to conceive than those without eating disorders. They were also more than twice as likely to seek fertility treatments in an effort to conceive a child.

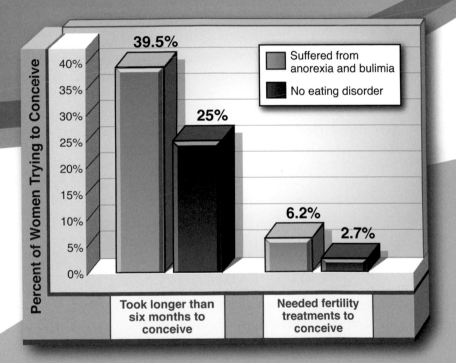

Source: King's College London, "Eating Disorders Linked to Fertility Problems and Unplanned Pregnancies," August 2011. www.kcl.ac.uk.

- According to the Goldfields Women's Health Care Centre in Australia, people with bulimia often hate the way they look, feel **hopeless**, have problems expressing **anger**, and/or have a hard time controlling **impulsive behaviors**.

Can People Overcome Bulimia?

❝With professional treatment, the vast majority of individuals with bulimia improve and many recover.❞

—Massachusetts General Hospital Harris Center, which is dedicated to the understanding, prevention, and treatment of eating disorders.

❝Although most people with bulimia do recover, some find that symptoms don't go away entirely.❞

—Mayo Clinic, a world-renowned medical facility headquartered in Rochester, Minnesota.

After struggling with bulimia for more than four years, Jessica Setnick finally reached rock bottom. One evening after dinner she was kneeling on the carpeted floor of her mother's bathroom—vomiting after yet another eating binge—when she was suddenly filled with disgust over what she was doing to herself. She recalls, "Where just moments before, I'd felt relief—pride, even—suddenly there was only despair. Sitting there, wasted from the effort of forcing myself to vomit for the umpteenth time that week, I was tired of doing this. Tired of hating myself that much." Setnick was about to enter graduate school to become a registered dietician, and the irony of that, in light of her recurrent bingeing and purging, was enough to push her in a drastically different direction. "It dawned on me that I was about to embark on a career where others would listen to my advice about food," she says. "Out loud I said, 'I don't want to live like this anymore.'"[56]

Convinced that with enough willpower she could conquer bulimia on her own, Setnick tried to quit bingeing and purging "cold turkey."

She soon learned, however, that she was only at the beginning of a very long journey toward recovery. One major challenge was keeping her mind off the destructive behaviors that had long controlled her life. "Sometimes I had to drive around the block instead of going home," says Setnick, "because I knew where I would go as soon as I walked in the door. It took years to learn how to eat the

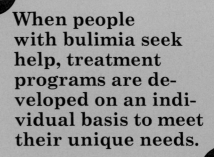

> When people with bulimia seek help, treatment programs are developed on an individual basis to meet their unique needs.

right amount, which helped lessen the temptation to vomit." One thing that shocked her was that she sometimes had a strong urge to vomit even when she had eaten nothing at all. "Throwing up," she says, "seemed to be a way of expressing bad feelings and trying to make them go away."[57]

Finding Her Calling

Setnick struggled on her own for six years before finally admitting that the only way she could truly heal was by seeking professional help. She began seeing a therapist who helped her address the emotional problems that had led to her developing bulimia. "I now understand why I needed my eating disorder, and also what I needed to let it go," she explains. When Setnick thinks about her years as a bulimic, she is convinced that the experience has helped her be a better dietician. As she counsels others who are fighting eating disorders, she understands—because she has been there. "In my practice," she says, "I use my experience to help women struggling with body-image issues to think more deeply about what's truly bothering them. . . . And as I help them find their own perfectly imperfect eating plans, I continue to work on accepting my own. We all want a flawless body, but sacrificing ourselves to get there just isn't worth it."[58]

The "Gold Standard" of Bulimia Treatment

When people with bulimia seek help, treatment programs are developed on an individual basis to meet their unique needs. Since a number of factors contribute to the disorder, the ideal treatment involves a team of professionals. This typically includes a physician who monitors the patient's health, one or more psychotherapists, and a dietician who provides the patient with nutrition counseling. The American Dietetic Association emphasizes that registered dieticians "are integral members of treatment teams and are uniquely qualified to provide medical nutrition therapy for the normalization of eating patterns and nutritional status."[59] Professional therapy is also an invaluable part of bulimia treatment because patients can address the underlying emotional issues that are at the root of their disorder.

One type of psychotherapy that has proved to be successful for people with bulimia is known as cognitive behavioral therapy (CBT), which is designed to help sufferers change unhealthy patterns of thinking. Referring to CBT as the "gold standard treatment for bulimia," psychologist John M. Grohol writes that "with the support of decades' worth of research, CBT is a time-limited and focused approach that helps [patients] understand how their thinking and negative self-talk and self-image can directly impact their eating and negative behaviors."[60] During CBT sessions, patients work on thinking more realistically rather than viewing every situation negatively. In the process they learn to identify and change irrational thoughts, attitudes, and beliefs that may trigger harmful behaviors such as bingeing and purging.

> "One type of psychotherapy that has proved to be successful for people with bulimia is known as cognitive behavioral therapy (CBT), which is designed to help sufferers change unhealthy patterns of thinking."

According to the National Eating Disorders Association, CBT for bulimics may be conducted on an individual basis or in a group. It usually involves sixteen to twenty hour-long sessions over a period of four to five months and is typically divided into three phases. The first phase focuses on educating patients about the dangers of their behavior, as well as teaching them strategies to resist urges to binge eat and purge. During the second phase, patients learn ways to reduce their self-imposed dietary limitations and increase the regularity of eating. The last phase involves learning relapse-prevention strategies to help them prepare for potential setbacks. The NEDA explains that "the goals of CBT are designed to interrupt the proposed bulimic cycle that is perpetuated by low self-esteem, extreme concerns about shape and weight, and extreme means of weight control."[61]

Getting Past the Shame

As effective as treatment can be for people with bulimia, most who suffer from it are never treated because they do not seek professional help. According to the National Association of Anorexia Nervosa and Associated Disorders, only one in ten people with eating disorders receives treatment. There are a number of reasons for failure to seek treatment, one of which is the shame, guilt, and embarrassment that bulimics feel over what they realize is abnormal behavior. It can be humiliating for them to admit to anyone that they gorge on food and then intentionally make themselves vomit. Unfortunately, such emotions often cause them to suffer in silence rather than getting the help they need.

For a long time this was the case with recovered bulimia sufferer Paula. Then, once she finally acknowledged that she needed help, she had no idea where to turn. "I couldn't fathom scheduling an appointment with my family doctor, who had treated me and everybody else in my family, to discuss this problem," she says. "Too risky. So I searched for something I could do on the basis of anonymity."[62] Paula finally worked up the courage to call a help line that had been created for students, and for the first time she confided in someone about her bulimia. When the woman told her that she was not alone, and

> As effective as treatment can be for people with bulimia, most who suffer from it are never treated because they do not seek professional help.

that laxative abuse was not uncommon, Paula was shocked. "I wanted to faint," she says. She was also surprised to learn that purging with laxatives was a growing trend among African American women. "That floored me again," she comments, "not only the fact that laxatives were a leading method for us, but that Black women had eating disorders! Not to find comfort in other people's pain, I felt . . . less shameful. I stopped feeling alone at that moment."[63]

The counselor urged Paula to admit herself to the hospital for an examination, which she did. Tests showed that she was critically dehydrated, had an irregular heart rate, and damaged intestines and esophagus. She was treated for three days in the hospital and then discharged with a follow-up recovery program, which included medically supervised weaning from laxatives and other substances that induce vomiting. The program also involved a healthy eating plan and weekly group support meetings, where Paula felt free to open up about the emotional roots of her eating disorder.

Over the following four months, Paula steadily improved until she no longer felt dependent on bingeing and purging. This recovery period was somewhat frightening at first because she started to gain weight, but she felt emotionally prepared to handle it. "A few pounds added to the scale were now the least of my worries," she says. "I just wanted to be free. If I could get to a normal state, emotionally and physically . . . maybe I would be able to focus on health and weight loss, in a non-destructive manner. . . . A few years later, I was able to do just that."[64]

A Valiant Fight

A tragic fact about bulimia is that not all sufferers are able to recover from it. According to a study published in July 2011 by researchers from the United Kingdom and Denmark, people with bulimia are twice as likely to die as individuals who do not have eating disorders. Even some who receive excellent treatment cannot overcome bulimia, which was the case with Melissa Avrin. She developed the disorder when she was thirteen years old, and she went out of her way to hide it from her family as long as she could. Eventually, however, her symptoms became too obvious to ignore—and by that time, she was consumed by the disorder. In an effort to keep Melissa from bingeing and purging, her mother took extreme precautions, such as leaving kitchen pantries bare and keeping food locked in trunks. But Melissa became so addicted that she would do anything to find food, even pawing through garbage cans outside on a freezing cold night. According to Judy Avrin, her daughter was "so in the grip of this eating disorder that she would consume anything. And if she did, it meant she would have to purge it."[65]

Melissa's parents sent her to a residential treatment program in Idaho, where she seemed to be making progress. According to her mother, "It's a wilderness program that works with kids with all kinds of problems, drinking and drugs and eating disorders. And by the end of—I believe it was six weeks—she was so incredibly proud of what she had accomplished. She rediscovered the joy of being healthy."[66] After Melissa's stay at the facility, her parents thought that she had turned a corner and was on her way to a complete recovery. Melissa then enrolled in a therapeutic boarding school, where she again seemed to be doing well. "She truly rediscovered the joy of her brain," says her mother. "She was incredibly bright, an amazing writer. She tutored other kids." But then, says Arvin, "the eating disorder came back in full force."[67]

Yet as sick as Melissa was, she never stopped believing that she would overcome bulimia. She had made plans to attend college and dreamed of someday becoming a filmmaker. Her steadfast belief about her eventual recovery was apparent in a poem she wrote, which her mother found after the girl's death: "Someday, I'll eat breakfast. I'll keep a job for more than three weeks. I'll have a boyfriend for more than 10 days. I'll love someone. I'll travel wherever I want. I'll make my family proud. I'll make a movie that will change lives."[68]

> " **According to a study published in July 2011 by researchers from the United Kingdom and Denmark, people with bulimia are twice as likely to die as individuals who do not have eating disorders.** "

Melissa was never able to travel or make her movie. She collapsed and died of a heart attack in May 2009, just before her eighteenth birthday. But as she had hoped, she indeed made her family proud because of how hard she fought the bulimia that consumed her life for so long. To honor her, and to raise awareness of the dangers of bulimia, the Avrins created a documentary called *Someday Melissa*. Their hope is that the film will save others from suffering the same tragic fate as the young woman for whom it is named. In that way, they will be fulfilling Melissa's wish to "make a movie that will change lives."

Reaching for a Better Tomorrow

Bulimia is a disorder for which there are tragic stories as well as happy endings. People who suffer from it can become so consumed by bingeing and purging that they feel their lives are controlled by an outside force. Reaching out for help is difficult, but those who do have a good chance of recovering if they are treated. According to many who have overcome bulimia, taking that first step—admitting they can no longer go on the way they have been—can be the key to a brand-new life. Shaye, a bulimia survivor, comments: "I never imagined that a life so full of happiness was possible. . . . A life so full of acceptance. . . . A life so uncomplicated, so simple. I especially never imagined that this type of life was possible for me."[69]

Primary Source Quotes*

Can People Overcome Bulimia?

66 **The thing about an eating disorder is that it's impossible to ever really be free from it.** 99

—Taylor Ellsworth, "My Toughest Addiction: Bulimia," *Salon*, March 11, 2012. www.salon.com.

Ellsworth suffered from numerous mental health conditions, including bulimia, throughout her young adult life.

66 **Recovery from a disorder as complex as bulimia is a process of successes, setbacks, realizations, and resolutions unique to each individual and without a well-defined ending.** 99

—Lindsey Hall and Leigh Cohn, *Bulimia: A Guide to Recovery*. Carlsbad, CA: Gürze, 2011, p. 103.

In 1980 Hall and Cohn wrote the first book on bulimia, which was based on Hall's struggle with the eating disorder and subsequent recovery from it.

66 **Often, people with bulimia are ashamed of their condition and do not ask for help for many years. By then, their habits are harder to change.** 99

—University of Maryland Medical Center, "Bulimia Nervosa," September 11, 2010. www.umm.edu.

The University of Maryland Medical Center is in partnership with the University of Maryland School of Medicine in Baltimore.

* Editor's Note: While the definition of a primary source can be narrowly or broadly defined, for the purposes of Compact Research, a primary source consists of: 1) results of original research presented by an organization or researcher; 2) eyewitness accounts of events, personal experience, or work experience; 3) first-person editorials offering pundits' opinions; 4) government officials presenting political plans and/or policies; 5) representatives of organizations presenting testimony or policy.

Primary Source Quotes

❝Someone with bulimia can get better. A health care team of doctors, nutritionists, and therapists will help the patient recover.❞

—Office on Women's Health, "Bulimia Nervosa," March 29, 2010. www.womenshealth.gov.

The Office on Women's Health is an agency of the US Department of Health and Human Services.

❝Eating disorders are real, treatable medical illnesses.❞

—National Institute of Mental Health, "What Are Eating Disorders?," 2011. www.nimh.nih.gov.

The National Institute of Mental Health is the largest scientific organization in the world dedicated to research focused on mental disorders and the promotion of mental health.

❝It is possible to recover from bulimia via therapy alone, but family participation will hasten recovery immensely. Families provide something that therapists, for all their care, cannot offer, and this is 24/7 LOVE.❞

—June Alexander, "Hope at Every Age (or Freedom: At Every Age)," National Eating Disorders Association, 2012. www.nationaleatingdisorders.org.

Alexander, who recovered from bulimia, is a journalist and the author of three books about her personal struggle.

❝Eating disorder specialists believe that the chance for recovery increases the earlier bulimia nervosa is detected.❞

—Susan Mendelsohn, "Bulimia Nervosa," Dr. Susie: Transform, Empower, Soar, 2011. www.transformempowersoar.com.

Mendelsohn is a certified clinical psychologist who works with patients who are battling eating disorders.

66 If you want to start your bulimia recovery, then start by believing in your mind that you can be a non-bulimic. 99

—Polly Mertens, "After 20 years—How Do I Overcome Bulimia?" EzineArticles.com, October 9, 2011. http://ezinearticles.com.

Mertens struggled with bulimia for twenty years and now runs her own website, help-with-bulimia.com, to provide information for others struggling with this disease.

66 The good news is, one of the most basic facts about bulimia and how to overcome it is simply admitting you have a problem and seeking help for it. 99

—Orchard Program, "Basic Facts About Bulimia and How to Overcome It," March 22, 2012. http://delraycenterforeatingdisordertreatment.com.

The Orchard Program is a treatment facility located in Delray Beach, Florida.

66 Recovery is about dealing with what's eating you, by feeling your emotions and feeding your true hunger. You may hunger for love, acceptance, comfort, peace, and confidence. 99

—Dorie McCubbrey, "Intuitive Solutions to Overcome Obesity and Eating Disorders," Positive Pathways, 2012. www.positivepathways.com.

McCubbrey is an eating disorder and obesity treatment specialist from Denver, Colorado.

Facts and Illustrations

Can People Overcome Bulimia?

- The National Institute of Mental Health says that **43.2 percent** of people with bulimia have sought treatment at some point during their lives.

- According to Cleveland Clinic psychiatrist Kathleen N. Franco, relapse rates for people treated for bulimia are between **30 and 50 percent** six months after treatment.

- The American Academy of Family Physicians states that nearly **50 percent** of patients who receive cognitive behavioral therapy are able to stop binge eating and purging.

- A 2011 analysis by the Agency for Healthcare Research and Quality found that hospitalizations for people diagnosed with eating disorders dropped **23 percent** between 2007 and 2009, which health officials believe is due to more sufferers being treated.

- According to a study published in July 2011 in the journal *Neuropsychopharmacology*, certain **genetic variations** in people who suffer from bulimia may complicate recovery.

- The Academy for Eating Disorders states that an estimated 50 percent of bulimia sufferers recover after treatment, **30 percent** show some improvement, and **20 percent** continue to be fully bulimic.

- According to a study published in June 2012 in the *Journal of Clinical Psychopharmacology*, more than **50 percent** of bulimia patients suffer from relapse.

Multifaceted Treatment

Eating disorder specialists emphasize that people who suffer from bulimia have an excellent chance of overcoming it if they receive individualized treatment, which is based on the patient's unique needs. Shown below are some of the most common methods of treating the disorder.

Psychotherapy	**Cognitive behavioral therapy (CBT):** Helps patient identify unhealthy, negative beliefs and behaviors and replace them with healthy, positive ones. **Interpersonal therapy:** Addresses difficulties in patient's close relationships, helping to improve communication and problem-solving skills. **Family-based therapy:** Helps parents intervene to stop their teenager's unhealthy eating behaviors; helps the teen regain control over his or her own eating; and helps the family deal with the problems bulimia can cause in the teen's development and in the family.
Nutrition counseling	Teaches the patient good nutrition to help him or her develop healthy eating behaviors and get back to normal weight.
Medications	Antidepressants may help reduce the symptoms of bulimia when used along with psychotherapy.
Alternative therapies (as complementary or supplemental treatments)	**Massage and therapeutic touch:** Helps reduce anxiety often associated with eating disorders. **Mind-body therapies** (such as meditation, yoga, biofeedback, and hypnosis): May increase awareness of the body's cues for eating and fullness, as well as promoting a sense of well-being and relaxation. **Acupuncture:** May help with anxiety and depression.

Source: Mayo Clinic, "Bulimia Nervosa," April 3, 2012. www.mayoclinic.com.

Most College Students Unwilling to Seek Treatment

A variety of treatments have proved to be successful in helping many people overcome bulimia. Studies have shown, however, that most sufferers do not reach out for help. To evaluate that problem among college students, the Eating Recovery Center conducted a survey of higher education professionals in March 2010. This graph shows how participants responded to questions about why students do not seek help for eating disorders.

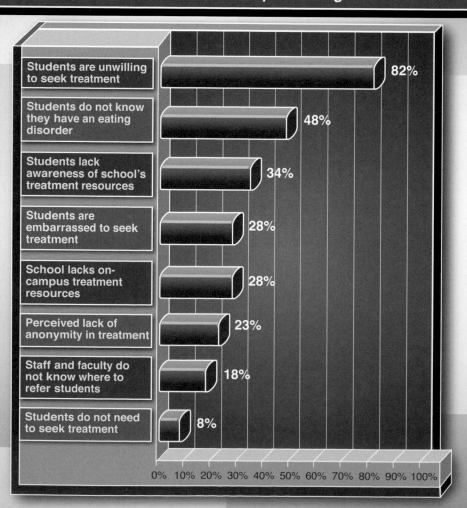

College staff and faculty perspectives on why students do not seek help for eating disorders

Students are unwilling to seek treatment	82%
Students do not know they have an eating disorder	48%
Students lack awareness of school's treatment resources	34%
Students are embarrassed to seek treatment	28%
School lacks on-campus treatment resources	28%
Perceived lack of anonymity in treatment	23%
Staff and faculty do not know where to refer students	18%
Students do not need to seek treatment	8%

0% 10% 20% 30% 40% 50% 60% 70% 80% 90% 100%

Source: *Eating Recovery Center* (blog), "Survey of Higher Education Professionals Shows Increase in Prevalence of Eating Disorders on Campus, Student Unwillingness to Seek Treatment," April 29, 2010. http://blog.eatingrecoverycenter.com.

Stress Linked to High Relapse Rate in Women

Research has shown that stressful life experiences make it hard for many people with disorders to fully overcome them. To examine this problem, a team of researchers followed the progress of 117 females who were in remission from either bulimia or eating disorder not otherwise specified. The team found that within six years nearly half of the bulimia sufferers relapsed, with the most significant stressors being relationships and work-related issues.

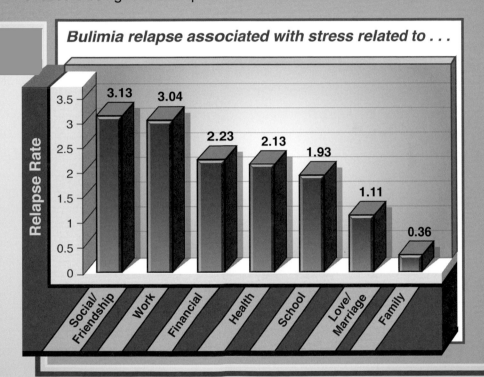

Bulimia relapse associated with stress related to . . .

The higher the number, the greater the effect of the stress-related factor on relapse.

Source: Carlos M. Grilo et al. "Stressful Life Events Predict Eating Disorder Relapse Following Remission: Six-Year Prospective Outcomes," *International Journal of Eating Disorders*, March 2012. www.ncbi.nlm.nih.gov.

- According to a 2010 article published in the *Journal for Specialists in Group Work*, behavioral therapy is effective for only **30 to 50 percent** of first-time bulimic patients.

Key People and Advocacy Groups

Amanda Beard: An Olympic swimmer who struggled with bulimia for years and wrote about her experience in a 2012 book called *In the Water They Can't See You Cry*.

Aaron Tempkin Beck: An American psychiatrist who is known as the father of cognitive behavioral therapy.

Cynthia Bulik: A clinical psychologist and well-known eating disorders specialist at the University of North Carolina, Chapel Hill School of Medicine.

Walter H. Kaye: A psychiatrist and program director of the Eating Disorders Program at the University of California, San Diego, who is known for his research on the relationship between brain chemistry and the development of bulimia and anorexia.

Steven Levenkron: A well-known New York City psychotherapist who specializes in eating disorders and has written a number of books on bulimia, anorexia, and self-injury.

James Lock: A professor of psychiatry and behavioral sciences at Stanford University's School of Medicine and a recognized authority on eating disorders.

Suzanne Mazzeo: A psychologist and noted eating disorders expert from Virginia.

National Association of Anorexia Nervosa and Associated Disorders: An organization that seeks to increase awareness of eating disorders and also serves as a resource center that provides information about eating disorders.

National Eating Disorders Association: A group whose goal is to expand public understanding and prevention of eating disorders, while promoting access to quality treatment and support for families through education, advocacy, and research.

David Rosen: A professor at the University of Michigan Medical School who is a well-known eating disorder specialist.

Gerald Russell: A British psychiatrist who was the first to formally recognize bulimia as an eating disorder in a 1979 paper entitled "Bulimia Nervosa: An Ominous Variant of Anorexia Nervosa."

Chronology

1903
In one of the earliest written accounts of eating disorders, French psychologist Pierre Janet publishes *Les Obsessions et la Psychasthénie*, a book in which he describes a patient named Nadja, who engaged in compulsive, secretive eating binges.

1980
The American Psychiatric Association formally recognizes bulimia as a mental illness in the revised third edition of the *Diagnostic and Statistical Manual of Mental Disorders*.

1973
German-born psychoanalyst Hilde Bruch publishes *Eating Disorders: Obesity, Anorexia Nervosa, and the Person Within*, which is one of the first books to explore the emotional aspects of eating disorders.

1900   **1960**   **1970**   **1980**

1966
Lesley Hornby, a seventeen-year-old British girl known as "Twiggy," rises to international fame as a supermodel; this profoundly changes the fashion world and popularizes skinny, waif-like bodies as the new feminine ideal.

1976
The National Association of Anorexia Nervosa and Associated Disorders is founded and becomes the first organization in the United States devoted exclusively to eating disorders.

1979
British psychiatrist Gerald Russell publishes a paper entitled "Bulimia Nervosa: An Ominous Variant of Anorexia Nervosa," in which he gives bulimia its name, and is the first to formally recognize it as an eating disorder.

1983
Popular recording artist Karen Carpenter dies of heart failure after a long battle with anorexia and bulimia; her autopsy report also shows that toxicity from syrup of ipecac, which she used to induce vomiting, was a factor in her death.

2000

A study by researchers from Paris, France, finds that 83 percent of participants with anorexia and 71 percent with bulimia also suffer from an anxiety disorder.

1984

In an interview with *Cosmopolitan* magazine, actress and physical fitness guru Jane Fonda admits that she struggled with bulimia for more than twenty years.

2011

A study by Sonja A. Swanson of the National Institute of Mental Health finds that the incidence of anorexia has been relatively stable since 1990, but bulimia and binge eating rates have nearly doubled.

1998

With the release of her autobiography, *Wasted: A Memoir of Anorexia and Bulimia*, author Marya Hornbacher draws public attention to the problem of eating disorders.

1990   2000   2010

2007

A study of three thousand adults is published in the journal *Biological Psychiatry* and reveals that one-fourth of eating disorder sufferers are men.

1992

Britain's Princess Diana publicly reveals that she suffers from bulimia; a later study by London's Institute of Psychiatry finds that reported cases of the illness rose dramatically during the 1990s after the princess's revelation.

2009

A study by the Agency for Healthcare Research and Quality finds that eating disorder–related hospitalizations for children under the age of twelve increased 119 percent between 1999 and 2006.

2012

Researchers from Tufts University in Boston publish a study that reveals a close connection between bulimia and substance addiction.

Related Organizations

Academy for Eating Disorders (AED)

111 Deer Lake Rd., Suite 100
Deerfield, IL 60015
phone: (847) 498-4274 • fax: (847) 480-9282
e-mail: info@aedweb.org • website: www.aedweb.org

The Academy for Eating Disorders is committed to being a leader in eating disorders research, education, treatment, and prevention. Articles and videos are available on its website, as well as a comprehensive eating disorders glossary.

Alliance for Eating Disorders Awareness

PO Box 2562
West Palm Beach, FL 33402-3155
phone: (866) 662-1235 • fax: (561) 841-0972
e-mail: info@eatingdisorderinfo.org
website: www.alllianceforeatingdisorderinfo.com

The Alliance for Eating Disorders Awareness provides educational information to parents and caregivers about the warning signs, dangers, and consequences of eating disorders. Plenty of good information about bulimia can be found in the "Eating Disorders Info" and "Getting Help" sections of its website.

American Academy of Child and Adolescent Psychiatry (AACAP)

3615 Wisconsin Ave. NW
Washington, DC 20016-3007
phone: (202) 966-7300 • fax: (202) 966-2891
e-mail: info@aacap.org • website: www.aacap.org

The AACAP is a professional medical association whose seventy-five hundred members actively research, evaluate, diagnose, and treat psychiatric disorders. Numerous articles about eating disorders can be accessed through the website's search engine, including a collection of fact sheets that are available in English and seven other languages.

Andrea's Voice Foundation

PO Box 2423
Napa, CA 94558
phone: (707) 224-8032
e-mail: doris@andreasvoice.org • website: www.andreasvoice.org

This organization was founded by the mother of a teenage girl who died from complications of bulimia. Its website offers a variety of educational materials about eating disorders.

Center for the Study of Anorexia and Bulimia (CSAB)

1841 Broadway, 4th Floor
New York, NY 10023
phone: (212) 333-3444 • fax: (212) 333-5444
e-mail: csab@icpnyc.org • website: http://csabnyc.org

The Center for the Study of Anorexia and Bulimia is devoted to treating individuals with eating disorders and training professionals who work with them. The "Eating Disorders 101" section of its website provides information on all eating disorders as well as links to other resources.

Eating Disorders Coalition for Research, Policy, and Action (EDC)

720 Seventh St. NW, Suite 300
Washington, DC 20001
phone: (202) 543-9570
e-mail: manager@eatingdisorderscoalition.org
website: www.eatingdisorderscoalition.org

The Eating Disorders Coalition for Research, Policy, and Action seeks to advance federal recognition of eating disorders as a public health priority. Its website offers articles about eating disorders, updates on research projects, information on federal policy, and a list of congressional briefings.

Families Empowered and Supporting Treatment of Eating Disorders (FEAST)

PO Box 331
Warrenton, VA 20188
phone: (540) 227-8518
e-mail: info@Feast-ed.org • website: www.feast-ed.org

FEAST is an international organization whose goal is to help people recover from eating disorders by providing information and support, promoting evidence-based treatment, and advocating for research and education. Numerous articles are available on its website, along with video and audio presentations, and an online forum.

National Association of Anorexia Nervosa and Associated Disorders (ANAD)

PO Box 640
Naperville, IL 60566
phone: (630) 577-1333 • helpline: (630) 577-1330
e-mail: anadhelp@anad.org • website: www.anad.org

The National Association of Anorexia Nervosa and Associated Disorders seeks to prevent and alleviate the problems of eating disorders. Its website offers a quarterly newsletter, a number of informative fact sheets, a "Males & Eating Disorders" section, and news articles.

National Association for Males with Eating Disorders (N.A.M.E.D.)

118 Palm Dr., #11
Naples, FL 34112
phone: (239) 775-1145; toll-free: (877) 780-0080
e-mail: Chris@NAMEDinc.org • website: www.namedinc.org

The National Association for Males with Eating Disorders seeks to provide support to men and boys who suffer from eating disorders while also educating the public and being an information resource. Its website provides statistics, articles about eating disorders, and information about prevention and treatment.

National Eating Disorder Information Centre (NEDIC)

ES 7-421, 200 Elizabeth St.
Toronto, ON, Canada M5G 2C4
phone: (416) 340-4156; toll-free (866) 633-4220 • fax: (416) 340-4736
e-mail: nedic@uhn.on.ca • website: www.nedic.ca

The National Eating Disorder Information Center provides information and resources on eating disorders as well as on food and weight preoccupation. The group also keeps the public informed about eating disorders and related issues. Its website offers fact sheets, news articles, and statistics about bulimia and other eating disorders.

National Eating Disorders Association (NEDA)

165 W. Forty-Sixth St., Suite 402
New York, NY 10036
phone: (212) 575-6200
e-mail: info@nationaleatingdisorders.org
website: www.nationaleatingdisorders.org

The National Eating Disorders Association works to prevent eating disorders and provides treatment referrals to those suffering from them. Its website offers position statements, news releases, resources for bulimia sufferers and families, and research papers.

National Institute of Mental Health (NIMH)

Science Writing, Press, and Dissemination Branch
6001 Executive Blvd., Room 8184, MSC 9663
Bethesda, MD 20892-9663
phone: (301) 443-4513; toll-free: (866) 615-6464 • fax: (301) 443-4279
e-mail: nimhinfo@nih.gov • website: www.nimh.nih.gov

An agency of the US government, the NIMH is the largest scientific organization in the world specializing in mental illness research and the promotion of health. Its website features statistics, archived *Science News* articles, and numerous publications accessible through its search engine.

For Further Research

Books

Stephanie Covington Armstrong, *Not All Black Girls Know How to Eat: A Story of Bulimia*. Chicago: Chicago Review, 2009.

Amanda Beard with Rebecca Paley, *In the Water They Can't See You Cry*. New York: Touchstone, 2012.

Lindsey Hall and Lee Cohn, *Bulimia: A Guide to Recovery*. Carlsbad, CA: Gürze, 2011.

Kathryn Hansen, *Brain Over Binge*. Phoenix: Camellia, 2011.

Joanna Poppink, *Healing Your Hungry Heart*. San Francisco: Conari, 2011.

Johanna S. Kandel, *Life Beyond Your Eating Disorder*. New York: Harlequin, 2010.

Lisa M. Schab, *The Bulimia Workbook for Teens*. Oakland, CA: Instant Help, 2010.

Carol Sonenklar, *Anorexia and Bulimia*. Minneapolis: Twenty-First Century, 2010.

Periodicals

Alexis Chiu, "Candace Cameron Bure: My Secret Battle," *People*, January 17, 2011.

Liza Ghorbani, "My Secret Life," *Marie Claire*, April 2012.

Bethany Heitman, "2 Demi Lovato: Outspoken. Brutally Honest. Undeniably Fearless," *Cosmopolitan*, July 2012.

Marina Khidekel, "Can You Catch an Eating Disorder?," *Seventeen*, March 2010.

Anne Kingston, "The Weight Debate: The Pressure to Be Thin Is True for a Duchess and Women in the Public Eye," *Maclean's*, July 25, 2011.

Kathleen McGuire, "Food Obsessed? The Dangerous Line Between Order and Disorder," *Dance,* October 2010.

Julie Mehta, "An Equal-Opportunity Destroyer: Meet Some Young Men Who Want You to Know the Truth About Eating Disorders," *Current Health 2,* February 2010.

New Moon Girls, "The Truth About Size: Boost Your Body Confidence," May/June 2010.

Christine Richmond, "What Eating Disorders Do to Your Body," *Glamour,* March 2010.

Internet Sources

American Psychological Association, "Eating Disorders," October 2011. www.apa.org.

Office on Women's Health, "An Interview About Eating Disorders: Krista Barlow," US Department of Health and Human Services, April 30, 2012. www.womenshealth.gov.

Taylor Ellsworth, "My Toughest Addiction: Bulimia," *Salon,* March 11, 2012. www.salon.com.

Chrissie Giles, "A Burst from the Blue: Is Bulimia Nervosa Really a Modern Disease?" Wellcome Trust, February 20, 2012. www.wellcome .ac.uk.

Charlotte Kemp, "The Secret World of Mid-Life Bulimics," *Daily Mail* (UK), September 2011. www.dailymail.co.uk.

Lavinia Rodriguez, "Breaking Free from Bulimia's Cycle of Bingeing and Purging," Mind over Fat Matters, May 8, 2012. www.fatmatters.com.

Melinda Smith and Jeanne Segal, "Bulimia Nervosa," Helpguide.org, July 2012. www.helpguide.org.

Source Notes

Overview

1. Quoted in Sasha Bronner, "Lady Gaga Is Surprise Guest at Young Women's Conference Who Talks Bullying, Bulimia, and Growing Up," *Huffington Post*, February 7, 2012. www.huffingtonpost.com.
2. Quoted in Bronner, "Lady Gaga Is Surprise Guest at Young Women's Conference."
3. Jessica Setnick, "An RD Confesses: 'I Had Bulimia,'" *Fitness*, 2009. www.fitnessmagazine.com.
4. April Uffner, "The Vicious Cycle of Bulimia," Yahoo! Voices, July 2, 2012. http://voices.yahoo.com.
5. Taylor Ellsworth, "My Toughest Addiction: Bulimia," *Salon*, March 11, 2012. www.salon.com.
6. American Psychological Association, "Eating Disorders," Psychology Topics, October 2011. www.apa.org.
7. Uffner, "The Vicious Cycle of Bulimia."
8. Office on Women's Health, "Bulimia Nervosa," US Department of Health and Human Services, June 15, 2009. www.womenshealth.gov.
9. American Psychological Association, "Eating Disorders."
10. National Institute of Mental Health, *Eating Disorders*, 2011. www.nimh.nih.gov.
11. Office on Women's Health, "An Interview About Eating Disorders: Kristina Barlow," US Department of Health and Human Services, April 30, 2012. www.womenshealth.gov.
12. National Association of Anorexia Nervosa and Associated Disorders, "General Information," 2012. www.anad.org.
13. National Eating Disorders Association, *The Media, Body Image, and Eating Disorders*, 2005. www.nationaleatingdisorders.org.
14. Princeton University Health Services, "Eating Disorders," April 18, 2012. www.princeton.edu.
15. Li Yan Wang, Lauren P. Nichols, and S. Bryn Austin, "The Economic Effect of Planet Health on Preventing Bulimia Nervosa," *Archives of Pediatric Adolescent Medicine*, August 2011, p. 756.
16. Lavinia Rodriguez, "Breaking Free from Bulimia's Cycle of Bingeing and Purging," Mind over Fat Matters, May 8, 2012. www.fatmatters.com.
17. National Institute of Mental Health, *Eating Disorders*.

What Is Bulimia?

18. Quoted in Chrissie Giles, "A Burst from the Blue: Is Bulimia Nervosa Really a Modern Disease?," Wellcome Trust, February 20, 2012. www.wellcome.ac.uk.
19. Quoted in Giles, "A Burst from the Blue."
20. Quoted in Giles, "A Burst from the Blue."
21. Quoted in Giles, "A Burst from the Blue."
22. Quoted in Giles, "A Burst from the Blue."
23. Melinda Smith and Jeanne Segal, "Bulimia Nervosa," HelpGuide.org, July 2012. www.helpguide.org.
24. Erin N. Umberg et al. "From Disordered Eating to Addiction: The 'Food Drug' in Bulimia Nervosa," *Journal of Clinical Psychopharmacology*, June 2012, p. 376.
25. Umberg et al. "From Disordered Eat-

ing to Addiction," p. 378.

26. Marcia Herrin, "Boys at Risk," In *The Parent's Guide to Eating Disorders.* Carlsbad, CA: Gürze, 2010. www.bulimia.com.

27. Herrin, "Boys at Risk."

28. Herrin, "Boys at Risk."

29. Quoted in Sam Jones, "'I Took Refuge in Stuffing My Face . . .'; John Prescott Admits Bulimia," *Guardian* (London), April 20, 2008. www.guardian.co.uk.

30. Quoted in *Harvard Women's Health Watch*, "Disordered Eating in Midlife and Beyond," February 2012. www2.massgeneral.org.

31. Quoted in Charlotte Kemp, "The Secret World of Mid-Life Bulimics," *Daily Mail*, September 2011. www.dailymail.co.uk.

32. Quoted in Kemp, "The Secret World of Mid-Life Bulimics."

What Causes Bulimia?

33. Paula, "Disordered: My Battle with Bulimia," *Madame: The Journal of a Weight Loss*ista* (blog)," February 2011. www.madamethejourneyblog.com.

34. Paula, "Disordered."

35. Stephen M. Mathis, "Adolescent Athletes," *COPE Today's Blog*, August 3, 2010. http://copetoday.wordpress.com.

36. Quoted in Melissa Rohlin, "Leaving the Sport, Gaining an Eating Disorder," *Los Angeles Times*, July 28, 2011. http://articles.latimes.com.

37. Quoted in GoodTherapy.org, "New Study Finds Self-Criticism to Be a Risk Factor for Bulimia in Adolescents," *Therapy News* (blog), December 16, 2011. www.goodtherapy.org.

38. Quoted in Johanna S. Kandel, *Life Beyond Your Eating Disorder.* New York: Harlequin, 2010, p. 32.

39. Quoted in Kandel, *Life Beyond Your Eating Disorder*, p. 32.

40. Suzanne E. Mazzeo and Cynthia M. Bulik, "Environmental and Genetic Risk Factors for Eating Disorders: What the Clinician Needs to Know," *Child and Adolescent Psychiatry*, January 2009. www.ncbi.nlm.nih.gov.

41. Quoted in Michigan State University news release, "MSU Researchers Discover Potential Genetic Factor in Eating Disorders," June 4, 2010. http://research.msu.edu.

42. Mazzeo and Bulik, "Environmental and Genetic Risk Factors for Eating Disorders."

43. Mazzeo and Bulik, "Environmental and Genetic Risk Factors for Eating Disorders."

44. Quoted in Alice Park, "How Social Networks Spread Eating Disorders," *Time* Health, "Healthland," January 7, 2011. http://healthland.time.com.

What Are the Risks of Bulimia?

45. Christina, "My Struggle with Bulimia," *Never the Skinny Girl* (blog), February 11, 2011. http://neverthe skinnygirl.blogspot.com.

46. Benjamin Wedro, "Electrolytes," WebMD eMedicine Health, September 29, 2010. www.emedicinehealth.com.

47. Quoted in *Daily Mail* (UK), "Bulimia Father Dies Aged 21 After Bullies' Cruel Taunts Drove Him to Shed TEN Stone," June 18, 2010. www.dailymail.co.uk.

48. Quoted in Sara Nathan, "Years of Crash Diets Left Me Infertile, Says Reality TV Star Chantelle Houghton," *Daily Mail* (UK), July 19, 2011. www.dailymail.co.uk.

49. National Eating Disorders Association, "Eating Disorders & Pregnancy: Some Facts About the Risks," 2005. www.nationaleatingdisorders.org.

50. Office on Women's Health, "Bulimia

Nervosa."

51. Lisa R. Cohen et al. "Survey of Eating Disorder Symptoms Among Women in Treatment for Substance Abuse," *American Journal of Addiction*, 2010. www.ncbi.nlm.nih.gov.

52. Cohen et al. "Survey of Eating Disorder Symptoms Among Women in Treatment for Substance Abuse."

53. Ellsworth, "My Toughest Addiction."

54. Recovery Ranch, "Long Term Effects of Bulimia," 2012. www.recoveryranch .com.

55. Quoted in *Science Daily*, "**Eating Disorders Impact Brain Function, New Brain Research Suggests**," July 13, 2011. www.sciencedaily.com.

Can People Overcome Bulimia?

56. Setnick, "An RD Confesses."

57. Setnick, "An RD Confesses."

58. Setnick, "An RD Confesses."

59. American Dietetic Association, "Position of the American Dietetic Association: Nutrition Intervention in the Treatment of Eating Disorders,"

Journal of the American Dietetic Association, August 2011, p. 1236.

60. John M. Grohol, "Treatment for Bulimia," PsychCentral, July 2012. http:// psychcentral.com.

61. National Eating Disorders Association, "Common Myths About Eating Disorders," *NEDA Toolkit for Coaches and Trainers*, August 2010. www.nati onaleatingdisorders.org.

62. Paula, "Disordered."

63. Paula, "Disordered."

64. Paula, "Disordered."

65. Quoted in Jacki Lyden, "Mother Speaks Out After Losing Daughter to Bulimia," NPR, April 2, 2012. www .npr.org.

66. Quoted in Lyden, "Mother Speaks Out After Losing Daughter to Bulimia."

67. Quoted in Lyden, "Mother Speaks Out After Losing Daughter to Bulimia."

68. Quoted in Lyden, "Mother Speaks Out After Losing Daughter to Bulimia."

69. Shaye, "My Bulimia Battle and Recovery," *Medusa* (blog), January 10, 2011. www.2medusa.com.

List of Illustrations

Index

Note: Boldface page numbers indicate illustrations.

Index

About the Author

Peggy J. Parks holds a bachelor of science degree from Aquinas College in Grand Rapids, Michigan, where she graduated magna cum laude. An author who has written more than one hundred educational books for children and young adults, Parks lives in Muskegon, Michigan, a town that she says inspires her writing because of its location on the shores of Lake Michigan.